Collins

Work on your
Grammar
Intermediate **B1**

Collins

HarperCollins Publishers
The News Building
1 London Bridge Street
London SE1 9GF

First edition 2013

© HarperCollins Publishers 2013

ISBN 978-0-00-749962-5

Collins® is a registered trademark of HarperCollins Publishers Limited

www.collinselt.com

A catalogue record for this book is available from the British Library

Typeset in India by Aptara

Printed and bound by CPI Group (UK) Ltd, Croydon, CR0 4YY

The material in this book has been written by a team from Language Testing 123, a UK-based consultancy that specializes in English language assessment and materials. The units are by Dittany Rose and have been based on material from the Collins Corpus and the Collins COBUILD reference range.

www.languagetesting123.co

Contents

Introduction 5
    Is this the right book for me? 5
    What does this book contain? 5
    I'm a student: how can I use this book? 6
    Study tips 6
    I want to improve my grammar 7
    I'm a teacher: how can I use this book with my classes? 8
    Lesson plan 8

1 Past simple, present perfect and present perfect continuous
Talking about the past and present together
(Past simple: verb + -*ed*)
(Present perfect: *has/had* + verb + -*ed*)
(Present perfect continuous: *has/have* + *been* + verb + -*ed*) 10

2 Past perfect, past perfect continuous and present perfect continuous
Talking about different times in the past and present
(Past perfect: *had* + verb + -*ed*)
(Past perfect continuous: *had* + *been* + verb + -*ing*) 13

3 Modals and passives
Using passives to show opinions about events and
situations (*have to*, *used to*, *be going to*) 17

4 *It* sentences
Using *it* to begin sentences and clauses (*It* + *be* +
adjective/noun/verb phrase + infinitive) 22

5 Reporting statements and imperatives
Reporting what people have said and commands 25

6 Reporting questions
Reporting questions people have asked 29

7 Modals (1)
Modals for making predictions with certainty
(*will/shall* and *be* + *going to*) 32

8 *Used to*
Using *used to* to talk about past situations (*used to* + verb) 35

9 Modals (2)
Talking about what you can and must do (*must, mustn't,
need, needn't, don't need, don't have to, have to*) 38

10 Modals (3)
Talking about events you are not sure about
(*must/can't/could/might* + *be*) 42

11 Showing how certain you are about situations 45

12 **Second and third conditionals**
Second conditional: *If* + past simple + *would* + present simple
Third conditional: *If* + past perfect + *would have* + past participle   49

13 **Conditionals**
as if, as though, as long as, provided, provided that   53

14 **Present simple and present perfect in future time**
Using present verbs to talk about the future   58

15 **Adverbs**
Words that add information about when, how often and how
things happen (*still, yet, any longer, any more, even, only*)   61

16 **Asking for, giving and refusing permission**
can, could, may   65

17 **Comparatives**
Making comparisons of people and things (*than, so …
as, as … as, much, not much*)   69

18 **Adjective order**
Using adjectives in the correct order to describe
people and things   72

19 ***-ing/-ed* adjectives**
Adjectives made from parts of verbs (*exciting/excited,
amazing/amazed, embarrassing/embarrassed*, etc.)   75

20 **Using *-ing* forms as nouns**   78

21 **Nouns and indefinite pronouns + *to-infinitive***
Using nouns and verbs to make subjects   81

22 ***wh-*clauses**
Using phrases with *wh*-pronouns to make objects
(*where, who, why, which, how, what*)   84

23 **Relative pronouns**
Using *wh*-pronouns when giving more information about
people and things (*who, which, that, whose, when, where*)   87

24 ***Have/get something done***
Talking about actions you arrange for other people to take   91

25 **Verbs that are used together**
Hear, see, want, need (*hear/see/want/need* + -ing, *hear/see* +
object + verb)   94

26 **Prepositions**
Prepositions for talking about the purpose of actions or things
(*for, with, as well as, rather than, except for, besides, apart from*)   98

27 ***Some/any/nobody/so/such***   102

28 ***The* in place names**
Names for places including *the*   106

29 **Verbs + *to* or *-ing***
Using *to* or *-ing* after verbs to make different meanings   109

30 **Giving short answers to questions**
so and *neither*   113

Answer key   117

Introduction

Welcome to *Work on your Grammar – Intermediate (B1)*.

Is this the right book for me?

This book, *Work on your Grammar – Intermediate (B1)*, helps students to learn and practise English grammar at CEF level B1. This book is suitable for you to use if you are at CEF level B1, or just below.

So, what is CEF level B1? Well, there are six Common European Framework levels. They go up from A1 for beginners, A2, B1, B2, C1 and finally C2.

If the description below sounds like you, then this is probably the right book for you. If not, choose *Work on your Grammar – Pre-intermediate (A2)* (below this level) or *Work on your Grammar – Upper Intermediate (B2)* (above this level).

- I can understand what people say and write about most regular activities, at school or college or work, at home, and so on.

- I can speak and understand enough English to travel in countries where English is spoken.

- I can express some of my opinions, with reasons, although I know I make quite a lot of mistakes.

- I need people to talk a little bit slowly to me.

- I think I know quite a lot of grammar, but I often get confused about it.

What does this book contain?

This book contains 30 units to help you learn and practise important grammar for this intermediate (B1) level.

Each unit explains the **grammar point** and then there is a series of **exercises** that give you useful practice in this particular area. The exercises are there to help you really understand the grammar point and how to use it correctly. There are different types of exercise. This helps you to see different aspects of the grammar, and it means you have a range of practice to do.

The **answers** to all the exercises are at the back of the book.

Remember! boxes highlight important information about the grammar points, so it is a good idea to read them and think about them.

I'm a student: how can I use this book?

You can use this book in different ways. It depends on your needs, and the time that you have.

- If you have a teacher, he or she may give you some advice about using the book.

- If you are working alone, you may decide to study the complete book from beginning to end, starting with unit 1 and working your way through to the end.

- You might find that it is better to choose which units you need to study first, which might not be the first units in the book. Take control of what you learn and choose the units you feel are the most important for you.

- You may also decide to use the book for reference when you are not sure about a particular grammar point.

- You can find what you want to learn about by looking in the **Contents** page.

- Please note that, if you do not understand something in one Unit, you may need to study a unit earlier in the book, which will give you more information.

Study tips

1 Read the aim and introduction to the unit carefully.

2 Read the explanation. Sometimes, there is a short text or dialogue; sometimes there are tables of information; sometimes there are examples with notes. These are to help you understand the most important information about this grammar point.

3 Don't read the explanation too quickly: spend time trying to understand it as well as you can. If you don't understand, read it again more slowly.

4 Do the exercises. Don't do them too quickly: think carefully about the answers. If you don't feel sure, look at the explanation again. Write your answers in pencil, or, even better, on a separate piece of paper. (This means that you can do the exercises again later.)

5 Check your answers to the exercises in the back of the book.

6 If you get every answer correct, congratulations! Don't worry if you make some mistakes. Studying your mistakes is an important part of learning.

7 Look carefully at each mistake: can you now see why the correct answer is what it is?

8 Read the explanation again to help you understand.

9 Finally, if the unit includes a **Remember!** box, then try really hard to remember what it says. It contains a special piece of information about the grammar point.

10 Always return: come back and do the unit's exercises again a few days later. This helps you to keep the information in your head for longer.

I want to improve my grammar

Good! Only using one book won't be enough to really make your grammar improve. The most important thing is you!

Of course, you need to have a notebook, paper or electronic. Try these six techniques for getting the best from it.

- *Make it real*: It's probably easier to remember examples than it is to remember rules. Often, it's better to try to learn the examples of the grammar, not the explanations themselves. For example, rather than memorizing 'You can use the present simple to talk about the future', you should learn 'My holiday starts on Monday'.

- *Make it personal*: When you're learning a new structure or function, try to write some examples about yourself or people or places you know. It's easier to remember sentences about your past than someone else's! For example, 'I'm studying art this year'.

- *Look out*: Everything you read or hear in English may contain some examples of the new grammar you're learning. Try to notice these examples. Also, try to write down some of these examples, so that you can learn them.

- *Everywhere you go*: Take your notebook with you. Use spare moments, such as when you're waiting for a friend to arrive. Read through your notes. Try to repeat things from memory. A few minutes here and there adds up to a useful learning system.

- *Take it further*: Don't just learn the examples in the book. Keep making your own examples, and learning those.

- *Don't stop*: It's really important to keep learning. If you don't keep practising, you won't remember for very long. Practise the new grammar today, tomorrow, the next day, a week later and a month later.

I'm a teacher: how can I use this book with my classes?

The contents have been very carefully selected by experts from Language Testing 123, using the Common European Framework for Reference, English Profile, the British Council Core Inventory, the Collins Corpus and material created for *Collins COBUILD English Grammar*, *Collins COBUILD Pocket English Grammar* and *Collins COBUILD English Usage*. As such, it represents a useful body of knowledge for students to acquire at this level. The language used is designed to be of effective general relevance and interest to any learner aged 14+.

The exercises use a range of types to engage with students and to usefully practise what they have learnt from the explanation pages on the left. There are enough exercises for each unit that it is not necessary for students to do all the exercises at one sitting. Rather, you may wish to return in later sessions to complete the remaining exercises.

The book will be a valuable self-study resource for students studying on their own. You can also integrate it into the teaching that you provide for your students.

The explanations and exercises, while designed for self-study, can be easily adapted by you to provide useful interactive work for your students in class.

You will probably use the units in the book to extend, back up or consolidate language work you are doing in class. This means you will probably make a careful choice about which unit to work on at a particular time.

You may also find that you recommend certain units to students who are experiencing particular difficulty with specific language areas. Alternatively, you may use various units in the book as an aid to revision.

Lesson plan

1 Read the aim and introduction to the unit carefully: is it what you want your students to focus on? Make sure the students understand it.

2 Go through the explanation with your students. You may read this aloud to them, or ask them to read it silently to themselves. With a confident class, you could ask them to read some of it aloud.

3 If there is a dialogue, you could ask students to perform it. If there is a text, you could extend it in some way that makes it particularly relevant to your students. Certainly, you should provide a pronunciation model of focus language.

4 Take time over the explanation page, and check students' understanding using concept-checking questions. The questions will vary according to content, but they may be based on checking the time in verb tenses. For example, with the sentence, 'She came on the train that got here yesterday', you could ask, 'When did she arrive?'. This might elicit the correct answer 'yesterday' and the incorrect answer 'tomorrow', and you would know if your students understood the meaning of the past simple verb. Or you could ask, 'Where is she now?' and correct answers would include 'here' while incorrect answers would include 'on the train'.

5 Perhaps do the first exercise together with the class. Don't do it too quickly: encourage students to think carefully about the answers. If they don't feel sure, look together at the explanation again.

6 Now get students to do the other exercises. They can work alone, or perhaps in pairs, discussing the answers. This will involve useful speaking practice and also more careful consideration of the information. Tell students to write their answers in pencil, or, even better, on a separate piece of paper. (This means that they can do the exercises again later.)

7 Check their answers to the exercises in the back of the book. Discuss the questions and problems they have.

8 If the unit includes a **Remember!** box, then tell students to try really hard to remember what it says. It contains a special piece of information about the grammar point.

9 Depending on your class and the time available, there are different ways you could extend the learning. If one of the exercises is in the form of an email, you could ask your students to write a reply to it. If the exercises are using spoken language, then you can ask students to practise these as bits of conversation. They can re-write the exercises with sentences that are about themselves and each other. Maybe pairs of students can write an exercise of their own together and these can be distributed around the class. Maybe they can write little stories or dialogues including the focus language and perform these to the class.

10 Discuss with the class what notes they should make about the language in the unit. Encourage them to make effective notes, perhaps demonstrating this on the board for them, and/or sharing different ideas from the class.

11 Always return: come back and repeat at least some of the unit's exercises again a few days later. This helps your students to keep the information in their heads for longer.

1

Past simple, present perfect and present perfect continuous

Talking about the past and present together

Past simple: verb + -ed

Present perfect: has/had + verb + -ed

Present perfect continuous: has/have + been + verb + -ed

In this unit you learn how to talk about events that happened in the past and also about the present effects of past events.

Past simple

You use the past simple for events that happened in the past. The past simple of a regular verb is formed by adding **-ed** to the base form of the regular verb.

> *My son **opened** his present and **smiled** at me.*
> *I **climbed** over the fence as fast as I could.*

If you are talking about the general past, or about regular or habitual actions in the past, you also use the past simple.

> *She **lived** just outside London.*
> *We often **saw** his dog sitting outside his house.*

> ### Remember!
> There are also many verbs with irregular forms.
> *be = was/were*
> *become = became*
> *get = got*
> *give = gave*
> *go = went*
> *have = has/had*
> *say = said*
> *see = saw*
> *teach = taught*
> *wake = woke*
> *wear = wore*
> *write = wrote*

Present perfect

Present perfect simple

You use the present perfect when you want to talk about the present effects of something that happened at a time in the past, or that started in the past but is still continuing. The present perfect is formed by using the present simple of **have** and the **-ed** participle of the main verb.

> I **have walked** five miles already! (= I'm tired now)
> **Have** you **seen** this film yet? (= at any time until now)
> **Have** you really **lived** here for ten years? (= You still live here now)
> He **has worked** here since 1987. (= He still works here now)
> **Have** you ever **stolen** anything? (= at any time until now)
> He **has been** here since six o'clock. (= and he is still here)

Sometimes, the present effects are important because they are very recent.

> Karen **has** just **passed** her exams.
> I'm afraid I**'ve forgotten** my book.

Present perfect continuous

When you want to say that a recent event continued to happen for some time, you use the present perfect continuous. The present perfect continuous is formed by using the present simple of **have**, **been** and the **-ing** form of the main verb.

> She's **been crying**.
> I**'ve been working** hard all day.
> We**'ve been waiting** here since before two o'clock.

Exercise 1

Choose the correct word or phrase, as shown.

1 Have they **gone** / **go** home yet, do you know?

2 **Have** / **Did** you go away for the summer this year?

3 She's **been writing** / **written** 20 emails today and she's pleased they're finished.

4 I'm really very happy here. **I 've lived** / **I lived** here for a long time.

5 I **'m** / **'ve** been staying in Paris for a month or two and may stay longer.

6 When **had** / **did** you arrive? It's lovely to see you!

Exercise 2

Which sentences are correct?

1 They have been staying at that hotel the whole summer. ☑

2 Have you ever been eating Japanese food? ☐

3 Did you have a good time today? ☑

4 The children are tired because they haven't been sleeping. ☑

5 They've arrived early yesterday morning. ☐

6 We haven't been knowing Mark and Sue very long. ☑

Exercise 3

Are the highlighted words and phrases correct or incorrect in this text?

Hi everyone! Thanks for reading my blog. So happy that you're interested in what **I've been doing**. ☑ Can't believe **I've been** ☑ here a week already – it **didn't seem** ☐ that long because **I've been going** ☑ out all the time. I've been to the beach most days this week but **didn't go** ☑ today because I got a bit red yesterday. Stupid, I know! I should be more careful. So, what's been happening after the beach? I **ate** ☐ every night in the same restaurant – from the first evening until now – and I think I'll keep eating there. Lovely fish!

Exercise 4

Decide if the pairs of sentences have the same meaning, as shown.

1 A I've been cleaning the house for the last two hours. ☑
  B I've spent the last two hours cleaning the house.

2 A Have you been swimming at the pool recently? ☑
  B Have you swum at the pool recently?

3 A Mark has gone to work. ☒
  B Mark has been to work.

4 A They've finished eating already. ☑
  B They aren't still eating.

Exercise 5

Write the past simple or present perfect simple form of the verb in brackets to complete each sentence, as shown.

1 I live in New York and I ___*have studied*___ (study) here for years. I love studying here!

2 When we were children, we ___lived___ (live) with my grandparents.

3 I ___spoke___ (speak) very good French when I was at school, but it's not very good now.

4 For a long time, many years ago, I ___was___ (be) a really good swimmer.

5 What a terrible week! I ___'ve worked___ (work) for 50 hours and it's not the weekend yet!

6 I've visited a lot of different places in the world and last year I ___visited___ (visit) Peru.

Exercise 6

Match the two parts, as shown.

1 He's tried hard,   a I've been running.
2 Why's your face so red?   b enjoy seeing your parents at the weekend?
3 Did you   c he been doing recently?
4 What's   d hasn't he?
5 Where have   e you been?
6 Last year, I   f went to Mexico again.

2

Past perfect, past perfect continuous and present perfect continuous

Talking about different times in the past and present

Past perfect: *had* + verb + *-ed*

Past perfect continuous: *had* + *been* + verb + *-ing*

In this unit you learn more about how to talk about the past and about the present effects of past events.

A = Clare had been walking all morning.
B = Clare had walked a long way in the morning.
C = Clare is tired. She's just walked all the way here.

Past perfect

Past perfect simple

You use the past perfect when you are talking about the past and you mention something that happened at an earlier time. The past perfect is formed by using **had** and the *-ed* participle of the main verb.

*She **had walked** for miles that day. (= she had stopped walking)*
*Jonathan was about 20. He **had studied** French at university for two years before he left to get a job in a bank. (= he had stopped studying French)*

Past perfect continuous

You use the past perfect continuous when you are talking about something that had started at an earlier time in the past but was still continuing. The past perfect continuous is formed by using **had been** and the **-ing** participle of the main verb.

*Clare **had been walking** all morning. (= she was still walking)*
*Jonathan was about 20. He **had been studying** French at university for two years.*
(= he was still studying French)

> ### Remember!
>
> You use the present perfect to talk about past events that have a present effect, including things that have happened recently.
> *I'm sorry! Can you pay? I've **left** my wallet at home.*
> *I've **just been** to see the new Batman movie. It's great!*

Exercise 1

Choose the correct word or phrase.

1 You've run out of money again?! What **have / had** you been spending it all on?
2 **I've been calling / I'd called** her all morning but she hasn't answered the phone.
3 Jed **has been looking / had looked** for work for ages but he can't find anything suitable.
4 **I'd been / I've been** out shopping so I didn't know she'd called round.
5 Belle **hasn't been buying / hadn't bought** any cheese because she'd decided to go on a diet.
6 The crime rate in the city **had been / has been** slowly rising until they increased the number of police on the streets.

Exercise 2

Match the two parts.

1 What have you been doing? C
2 Mandy had been complaining about a pain in her leg. F
3 I hadn't been to visit my grandma for ages
4 Carl had been taking sailing lessons for a long time
5 Jibril has been working really hard on his English
6 I had already applied for the course

a when I decided to do something else instead.
b and he's pretty good now.
c You're covered in mud!
d so she was really pleased to see me.
e before he felt confident enough to go out on his own.
f I told her to go to the doctor's.

Exercise 3

Put the correct phrase in each gap, as shown.

| I'd been cleaning | What have you done | She had laughed | ~~I'd been sleeping~~ |
| I'd overslept | I'd missed | Have you been sleeping | She'd been joking |

It was late when I woke – [1] *I'd been sleeping* very heavily. The house was silent – no cat meowing for his breakfast, no sounds from the kitchen of my sister making her morning cup of coffee. I knew [2] *I'd overslept* and grabbed my phone to check the time. Half past eleven! It was the weekend, though, so I rolled over and snuggled back under the duvet.

Two hours later I heard someone calling my name. It was my sister, back from work. She came into my bedroom. '[3] ~~What~~ *Have you been sleeping* all this time?' she asked. 'You've missed Angela's wedding!' Oh no! [4] *I'd missed* the most important day of my friend's life! She would never forgive me. Perhaps I could get to the reception on time. I rushed downstairs and saw my sister smiling. 'What's so funny?' I demanded. 'The wedding's next week!' she said. [5] *She had been joking*

Later in the week, [6] *I'd been cleaning* the house and had found a small jumper that belonged to one of my old teddy bears. An idea came into my head. I washed some clothes and waited for my sister to come home. 'Erm, Caroline?' I said. I held up the teddy bear's jumper, which was almost the same as my sister's favourite sweater. 'I'm sorry but I washed the clothes too hot and . . .'

She's just about forgiven me now!

Exercise 4

Complete the text by writing one word in each gap.

It had [1] *been* a long day. I [2] ~~tried~~ *had* got up early in the morning to get ready for the marathon. I had [3] ~~tried~~ *been* training for months and had been [4] ~~appeared~~ *looking* forward to the big day. I warmed up with the others on the starting line and soon we were off! Everything was going really well until, suddenly, I tripped over someone's foot and broke my ankle! I [5] *had* had dreams of winning the race but instead [6] ~~feeling~~ *had* ended up in hospital with my leg in plaster! Maybe next year . . .

Exercise 5

Write the correct form of the verb in brackets to complete each sentence.

1 Hey, Trudie! What have you been *doing* (do)? I haven't seen you for ages!
2 Hadn't you *tried* (try) sushi before?
3 Josh ~~have you~~ *HAD* been studying hard, so he was disappointed with his results.
4 I'd never *appeared* (appear) on TV before, so I was quite nervous.
5 My children *have been* (have) been spending a lot recently, so I ought to make them start saving!
6 I'd been ~~felt~~ *feeling* (feel) a little lonely, so my friends took me out for dinner.

Exercise 6

Find the wrong or extra word in each sentence, as shown.

1 Archie realized he hadn't been ~~to~~ cycling for ages, so he decided to go that afternoon.

2 It hadn't stopped ~~on~~ raining for a month and everyone was really fed up.

3 Jo had forgotten to buy her daughter ~~the~~ computer game she wanted, even though she'd ~~been~~ put it on her shopping list.

4 You look hot! Have you ~~ever~~ been out running?

5 Morag hadn't uploaded ~~oh~~ her work ~~onto~~ the website and her teacher was really annoyed.

6 I haven't ~~not~~ been practising recently and I ~~can~~ hardly remember how to play my violin.

Exercise 7

Decide if the pairs of sentences have the same meaning.

1 A The government hadn't put taxes up for a while.
   B The government will not put taxes up yet. ☐

2 A The volcano hadn't erupted for years.
   B The volcano might erupt soon. ☐

3 A I'd been going to the gym for a long time and I had become really fit.
   B Going to the gym so often helped me to get very fit. ☑

4 A Lucie's been chatting online for hours – I wonder who she's talking to?
   B I want to know who Lucie is talking to – she's been online for a long time. ☑

5 A Employment had risen by two per cent by the end of last year.
   B More people have jobs now than at the end of last year. ☐

Exercise 8

Which sentences are correct?

1 Amy hadn't been interested in politics until she saw a programme explaining how new laws might affect her. ☑

2 The air-conditioning has been broken since March and the landlord wouldn't come to repair it. ☐

3 We hadn't realized that water had been dripping into the cellar. It's going to cost a lot to fix. ☑

4 Matt had written a really interesting article but the newspaper not published it. ☐

5 Elena had been feeling terrible since she'd been eaten some seafood. ☐

6 The live news channel had been on in our house since we'd heard about the disaster. ☑

3

Modals and passives

Using passives to show opinions about events and situations

> **have to, used to, be going to**

In this unit you learn how to change what you say so that it focuses on the person or thing that is affected by an action. You learn how to do this when you are using modal verbs and some other verb forms that can be used in a similar way.

Passive forms

The passive is made with the verb **be**, followed by the past participle of a main verb. In the following examples you will see how to use the passive with modal verbs.

The difference between passive and active

When you want to talk about the person or thing that performs an action, you use the active:

> *Mr Smith must lock the gate at 6 o'clock every night.*
> *The storm will destroy hundreds of trees.*

When you want to focus on the person or thing that is affected by an action, you use the passive:

> *The gate must be locked at 6 o'clock every night.*
> *Hundreds of trees will be destroyed.*

Using passive forms with modal verbs

Modal verbs only have one form. There is no **-s** form for the third person singular of the present simple, and there are no **-ing** or **-ed** forms. When they are followed by another verb it is always the base form of that verb.

The modal verbs are: **can**, **could**, **may**, **might**, **must**, **ought**, **shall**, **should**, **will** and **would**.

As you can see from the examples above, when you are talking about the present you use **be** followed by the **-ed** participle of a main verb:

> *What can **be done**?*
> *We won't **be beaten**.*

When you are talking about the past, you use **have been** followed by the past participle of a main verb:

> *He may **have been given** the car.*
> *He couldn't **have been told** by Jimmy.*

Remember!

Instead of using modals, you can often use other verbs and expressions.

When you want to say that there is an obligation to do something, or that it is necessary that something is done, you use **have to**.

*The bill **has to be paid** by Thursday.*

*The shopping **had to be done** before the party.*

If something 'used to be done', it happened regularly in the past, but doesn't happen now.

*Trams driven by horses **used to be seen** regularly in European cities.*

*Small boys **used to be sent** to work in mines and factories in awful conditions.*

When you are talking about the future, you can use **be going to**.

*He's too slow. He's **going to be beaten**.*

*This room still hasn't been tidied. But don't worry, it's **going to be done** tomorrow.*

Exercise 1

For each question, tick the correct answer, as shown.

1 Pay day was last week so he
- ☐ may have been paid by now.
- ☑ must have been paid by now.
- ☐ might have been paid by now.

2 Before she got too old, the horse
- ☐ used to be ridden for two hours a day.
- ☐ has to be ridden for two hours a day.
- ☐ is going to be ridden for two hours a day.

3 The plan is that a new hospital is going
- ☐ to be built on the site this year.
- ☐ to may be built on the site this year.
- ☐ to have been built on the site this year.

4 Dan's furious because he feels
- ☐ he may be promoted this year.
- ☐ he had to be promoted this year.
- ☐ he should have been promoted this year.

5 If you commit a serious crime and are caught by the police, you
- ☐ could have been arrested.
- ☐ will be arrested.
- ☐ may be arrested.

Exercise 2

Choose the correct word or phrase.

1 Your bags will **have been locked / lock / be locked** in a safe room until you are ready to leave the hotel.

2 In the UK, goose or turkey always used **to be eating / to be eaten / to eat** on Christmas day, but now people often have different types of meat.

3 Hard hats have **to wear / to be wearing / to be worn** on the building site at all times.

4 This project should **have been completed / be completed / be complete** last week but it was delayed.

5 Many schoolchildren believe they **should give / should have been given / should be given** less homework.

Exercise 3

Put the correct word in each gap.

can't | used | should | will | be | wouldn't | can

Creating a golden opportunity from misfortune

David Kiley could [1]_____ forgiven for feeling that he's had some bad luck in life. Paralysed from the waist down in an accident at the age of 19, he has spent the whole of his adult life in a wheelchair.

As a teenager, Kiley [2]_____ to dream of playing professional basketball and eventually getting his name into the basketball hall of fame. The accident made this impossible, but Kiley chooses to see what occurred as fate. He tells people to this day that he [3]_____ have been given the opportunity to compete in the Paralympics if the accident hadn't happened.

Having won nine gold medals at the Paralympics, Kiley's achievements [4]_____ be more widely recognized. Paralympians work extremely hard and devote as many hours to training as any sportsperson. Yet the profile of Paralympians such as Kiley has never been as high as that of the able-bodied Olympic athletes.

Kiley retired from basketball in 2000 and [5]_____ now be seen shouting from the sidelines of basketball courts as a successful coach. He was an assistant coach for the US Paralympic teams that played in 2004 in Athens, and the gold medal-winning team in Beijing in 2008.

But Kiley's career [6]_____ be confined to the world of basketball. For 17 years he worked at a rehabilitation centre in California, helping people with disabilities by getting them to play sport. Today, programmes like this are to be found around the world.

In decades to come, David Kiley's contribution to disabled sports [7]_____ be remembered by everyone that he has helped.

Exercise 4

Which sentences are correct?

1 The valuable ring may been lost on public transport but it's more likely that someone stole it. ❏
2 Meat from the freezer must defrosted thoroughly before it's cooked. ❏
3 The house is going to be sold at auction next Saturday. ❏
4 Children under the age of 16 have to be accompany by a responsible adult. ❏
5 That man should give a medal for bravery! I can't believe he went into a burning building to rescue those people. ❏
6 The treasure will be hidden in a secret place not far from here. ❏

Exercise 5

Decide if the pairs of sentences have the same meaning.

1 **A** Dave might have been asked to work late by his boss.
  B Dave's boss probably asked him to work late. ☐

2 **A** The shot can't have been fired from this gun as the bullet doesn't match.
  B It's unlikely that the bullet was fired from this gun as it doesn't match it. ☐

3 **A** The letter should have been sent to this address, not to where I used to live.
  B The letter was sent to the wrong address. ☐

4 **A** Milk has to be kept cold or it will go off.
  B It's a good idea to keep milk in the fridge. ☐

5 **A** The car's in great condition. It must have been kept in a garage.
  B To keep it in good condition, the car must be kept in a garage. ☐

Exercise 6

Find the wrong or extra word in each sentence.

1 A celebrity may to be offered a lot of money to write their autobiography.

2 That letter can't have be meant for you – it hasn't got your name on it.

3 Alexander should have to been taught English from an earlier age; it's harder to learn when you're older.

4 Tomorrow, the bride and groom will be being brought to the hotel by chauffeur-driven limousine.

5 Cassie should not to have been released from hospital today; she still feels unwell.

6 A complimentary ticket to our next event will have be given out to the first 200 people through the doors.

Exercise 7

Are the highlighted words correct or incorrect in the sentences?

1 The children should never **have** ☐ been allowed so much freedom.

2 You have to **have** ☐ been granted a special licence to drive this vehicle.

3 The dog's starving; it **mustn't** ☐ have been fed for days.

4 The boiler hasn't **had** ☐ to be repaired since we bought the house.

5 Uniform **hasn't** ☐ to be worn by pupils at the school; they can wear their own clothes if they want to.

6 Hurry up! The concert will have **been** ☐ finished before we arrive.

Exercise 8

Write the missing words in sentence B so that it means the same as sentence A, as shown.

1 **A** The artist may have spent the last years of his life in this house.
   B The last years of the artist's life _____*may have been spent*_____ in this house.

2 **A** It's a good idea to take out holiday insurance if you're going abroad.
   B Holiday insurance _____ if you're going abroad.

3 **A** Music societies used to hire the town hall for their performances.
   B The town hall _____ by music societies for their performances.

4 **A** It's possible to learn how to ski in a couple of weeks.
   B Skiing _____ in a couple of weeks.

Exercise 9

Complete the sentences by writing one word in each gap.

1 The rules say that protective glasses _____ to be put on when handling chemicals.

2 The style of the fireplace indicates that it may _____ been manufactured in the Victorian era.

3 Pete _____ use to be paid much but now he earns quite a lot.

4 Because her parents go away a lot, Sheila will _____ sent away to school.

5 Those shoes _____ have been worn more than twice – they look brand new.

6 Marc could _____ been woken by the sound of the milkman – or perhaps it was the birds.

Exercise 10

Write the correct passive form of the verb in brackets to complete each sentence.

1 I think it's great that books _____ (can) read on an e-book reader; it's much more convenient.

2 We haven't seen our cat for days. We think she _____ (may) stolen.

3 The song is _____ (going to) sung by the Welsh Male Voice Choir.

4 Money _____ (should) lent to friends because it ruins friendships.

5 Speedboats _____ (used to) allowed on this lake because the council thought they were too noisy.

6 The sound of the concert _____ (could) heard for miles around.

4

It sentences

Using *it* to begin sentences and clauses

It + *be* + (adjective/noun/verb) phrase + infinitive

In this unit you learn how to use **it** to begin sentences. You do this when you want to introduce new information, and **it** is used in particular when you talk about personal opinions. Using **it** in this way takes the focus off the subject.

Using *it* as the subject of a sentence

With an infinitive

You can use **it** to begin sentences when you want to describe an experience or comment on a situation. For example, instead of saying *Walking by the lake was nice*, you can say:

It was nice to walk by the lake.

Notice how the verb is in the **to** form:

*It's lovely **to hear** your voice again.*
*It was sad **to see** her in so much pain.*
*It was difficult trying **to talk** to her.*
*It's nice **to see** you with your books for a change.*

With *for* and an infinitive

If you want to mention the person who performs the action or has the experience, you use a phrase beginning with **for** and a **to**-*infinitive*.

It is hard for a shy child to develop confidence.
It's good for you to meet her, so you can talk about the plans.

> *Remember!*
>
> Don't use **it** to say that something exists or is present. Don't say, for example, ~~It's a lot of traffic on this road tonight~~.
> Say:
> **There's** *a lot of traffic on this road tonight.*

You can use **it** with a linking verb and an adjective to describe the experience of being in a particular place. After the adjective, you use a phrase referring to the place.

It's very quiet here.
It was warm in the restaurant.

Exercise 1

Write the missing words in sentence B so that it means the same as sentence A.

1 A It's fun to go out with friends.
  B _____ with friends is fun.

2 A Finishing on time will be difficult.
  B It'll be difficult _____ on time.

3 A Passing the exam wasn't easy for any of us.
  B _____ easy for any of us to pass the exam.

4 A Which is better, going today or going tomorrow?
  B _____ to go today or tomorrow?

Exercise 2

Decide if the pairs of sentences have the same meaning.

1 A It isn't very nice to be ill.
  B Being ill isn't very nice. ❏

2 A Kathy is an interesting person.
  B It was interesting to see Kathy. ❏

3 A Was it a good idea to spend so much on a new car?
  B Do you think spending so much on a new car was a good idea? ❏

4 A Wasn't seeing Richard again a surprise! ❏
  B Wasn't it a surprise to see Richard again!

5 A A foreign language may be hard to learn. ❏
  B It's sometimes hard to learn a foreign language.

Exercise 3

Choose the correct word or phrase.

1 It was great **to see / saw / see** you again last week.

2 It's **nice / nicer / nicest** outside today than it was yesterday.

3 It wasn't easy **me / to me / for me** to tell you the bad news.

4 In the past, it was easier for people **should eat / ate / to eat** healthy food.

5 People love sunny weather and it's good **for them / to them / for they** to go out and enjoy it.

Exercise 4

Choose the correct word or phrase.

Hi Sue

Having a wonderful time! It was a good idea ¹**came / come / to come** here again and it's really lovely for the children and me ²**are / is / to be** with Chris and Lucy in their beautiful house. It was a lovely day ³**go / to go / went** to the beach yesterday. Lucy said that it would be nice ⁴**to / for / with** her and Chris if you ⁵**will visit / going to visit / came to visit** next year.

Hope to see you when I get back.

John

Exercise 5

Put each sentence into the correct order, as shown.

1 for / it / play outside / was / possible / the children / to / ?
   Was it possible for the children to play outside?

2 good / it's / to be / working so hard / not / for you / .

3 be / them / it must / for / nice / to see / you again / .

4 on time / hard / for her / it / to finish / wasn't / .

5 it's / to / easier / much / for / me / do / that for you / .

6 always / isn't / for me / it / possible / to / call / .

Exercise 6

Which sentences are correct?

1 It's good for you to be exercising so much. ❏
2 It's really healthy for people eat lots of fruit and vegetables. ❏
3 It is usually hard for people to get tickets for that show. ❏
4 Was it a good idea for you arrive for the concert so early? ❏
5 Was it always easy for you to pass exams? ❏
6 Wasn't it nice for you to see them again? ❏

5

Reporting statements and imperatives

Reporting what people have said and commands

In this unit you learn how to report things that other people say. You can take what they say and put it in your own words.

Reporting statements

I want to go home.

Last week you went to a party with your friend Jim. At about 9 o'clock Jim decided to go home. When you tell a friend about the party the next day, you say:

> Jim **said** he **wanted** to go home. *I thought it was very early!*

Reported speech consists of two parts. One part is the reporting clause (**Jim said**), which contains the reporting verb, and the other part is the reported clause (**he wanted to go home**). Because reports are usually about something that was said or believed in the past, both the reporting verb and the verb in the reported clause are often in a past form.

Reporting commands

If you want to report an order or a piece of advice, you use a **to**-*infinitive* clause after a reporting verb such as **tell** or **advise**. You mention the hearer as the object of the verb, before the **to**-*infinitive* clause.

> I **told** Jim **to stay** *until 11 o'clock.*
> He **ordered** me **to fetch the books**.
> He **advised** me **to buy it**.

If the order, request or advice is negative, you put **not** before the **to**-*infinitive*:

*He had ordered his officers **not** to use any weapons.*
*Doctors advised him **not** to play for three weeks.*

When you report what someone says you may have to change references to times and places. This is because the original thing that was said happened in a different place and time.

If Justin said, '*I went there **yesterday**'*, you report this as:
He said he had been there **the previous day**.

If Lisa said, '*I'm going to Singapore **next year**'*, you report this as:
She said she was going to Singapore **the following year**.

If Alicia said, '*I like it **here**. I think I'll stay'*, you report this as:
Alicia said she liked it **there** and thought she would stay.

Exercise 1

Match the sentence halves.

1	We agreed	**a**	me for breaking the TV remote control.
2	My mum advised	**b**	on paying for the meal.
3	My brother blamed	**c**	me not to go out with Joe.
4	Michael insisted	**d**	for being rude.
5	Dave apologized	**e**	that she didn't like my boyfriend.
6	Caroline admitted	**f**	to watch the match at Zack's house.

Exercise 2

Put the correct word in each gap.

insisted | encouraged | promised | admitted | told | warned | suggested | explained

Hi Sonni

What a day! I know I ¹_____ not to complain about work anymore but I went for some careers advice this morning. They ²_____ that I filled in a questionnaire first of all. I had to tick loads of boxes to say what I liked and didn't like. They ³_____ me not to miss any out because otherwise the computer wouldn't be able to read my results properly. Anyway, after I'd finished the computer printed off a list of jobs it had matched me with and guess what it ⁴_____? The job I'm already doing! I ⁵_____ the careers adviser that it had been a waste of time but she ⁶_____ me to look at the other jobs on the list. I'm glad I did because I've found my dream job – training guide dogs for the blind!

See you later!

Trix

Exercise 3

Decide if the pairs of sentences have the same meaning.

1 **A** 'There's no way I'm going to Steve's leaving party,' George said.
   B George considered going to Steve's leaving party. ❑

2 **A** 'The Italian restaurant on the corner's worth trying,' he said.
   B He suggested trying the Italian restaurant on the corner. ❑

3 **A** 'Why don't you come round for a meal on Sunday?' Mick said.
   B Mick invited us to go round for a meal on Sunday. ❑

4 **A** 'Sit down this minute!' the teacher said.
   B The teacher encouraged us to sit down that minute. ❑

5 **A** 'If I were you, I'd take Maths at university,' Ella said.
   B Ella warned me to take Maths at university. ❑

Exercise 4

Are the highlighted words correct or incorrect in the sentences?

1 'It's your fault!' she **apologized** ❑.

2 Nigel **offered** ❑ me his jacket – I took it because it was freezing!

3 The doctor **advised** ❑ me not to go dancing while my foot was sore.

4 'Do you know where I can find the nearest cash machine?' she **told** ❑ me.

5 I've finally **reminded** ❑ where my keys are – thank goodness!

6 Bill said he wouldn't go to the concert with me – he absolutely **refused** ❑!

Exercise 5

Find the wrong or extra word in each sentence.

1 Steffi agreed not to go bungee jumping with me. I'm so glad we did it!

2 'Be careful with that hot coffee!' she warned to us.

3 Petra insisted on that we stayed for dinner.

4 Nicole suggested I going to the aerobics class with her.

5 Mum promised to go to shopping with me later that day.

6 Candice encouraged to her brother to buy the new car he wanted.

Exercise 6

Choose the correct word.

1 Sheila commented that there were more people at the conference than there had been **the previous / last** year.

2 Dad told me **this / that** was the last time he'd take me out for a driving lesson.

3 He told me that no one was sitting **here / there**.

4 Zohra insisted she'd switched off the computers **the previous day / yesterday**.

5 My brother invited us for dinner **next week / the following week**.

6 Terry had blamed me for writing on the desk **the day before / yesterday**.

Exercise 7

Put each sentence into the correct order.

1 bike / my / breaking / admitted / Andrew / .

_____

2 job / told / they / the / me / got / hadn't / I / .

_____

3 barbecue / Penelope / to / the / not / decided / go / to / .

_____

4 me / Bradley / agreed / go / hospital / the / to / to / with / .

_____

5 what / Pat / said / he / apologized / for / had / .

_____

6 a / waiter / recommended / the / wine / good / .

_____

Exercise 8

Complete the sentences by writing one word in each gap.

| not | on | to | me | that | me |

1 The scientist explained _____ it was important to analyse the data carefully.

2 Jed blamed _____ for leaving the tap running, but I didn't.

3 The dentist advised _____ to brush my teeth more often.

4 I've decided _____ to go to university. It's too expensive.

5 My sister promised _____ help me with my homework, but she didn't.

6 The teacher insisted _____ good behaviour on the class trip.

Exercise 9

Choose the correct word or phrase.

3 October: First day at university

Had a great first day at uni. Made some new friends, Rob and Mel. Mel's on the same course as me and Rob [1]**told / said** me he was studying Engineering. Sounds really hard. We've agreed [2]**to meet / meeting** for coffee before classes start tomorrow.

Met the course tutors as well today. They [3]**explained us / explained** the timetable and showed us where their offices were. They also [4]**reminded us / reminded** of how important it is to get work in on time and suggested [5]**to take / taking** a look at the relevant section of the library to find the books we'd need.

Bit nervous about starting classes but I know someone in the second year and she promised [6]**help / to help** me if I need anything. Off to bed now.

6

Reporting questions
Reporting questions people have asked

In this unit you learn how to report questions that people have asked you.

Questions with *wh*-words

Last week you went to a party with your friend Jim. He decided to leave the party at 9 o'clock. You said to Jim, *'Why are you leaving so early?'* When you tell another friend about this you say:

*I **asked** Jim **why he was leaving** so early.*

Reported questions consist of two parts. One part is the reporting clause (**I asked Jim**), which contains the reporting verb, and the other part is the reported clause (**why he was leaving so early**). When you are reporting a question, the verb in the reported clause is often in a past form. This is because you are often talking about the past when you are reporting someone else's words.

In reported questions, the **subject** of the question comes before the verb:

***She** asked me what I was doing.*
***He** wanted to know what my name was.*
***I** demanded to know where I was going.*

Yes/No questions

You do not normally use the auxiliary **do** in reported questions. Instead, you use **if** or **whether** to introduce reported **yes/no** questions. So to report the question *Do your parents speak French or German?* you say:

*She asked me **if** my parents spoke French or German.*

To report the question *Are you single?* you say:

*I asked him **whether** he was single.*

Reporting clause	Reported clause
She asked me	if/whether my parents spoke French.
He wanted to know	why I was leaving so early.
I asked him	what his name was.
He asked her	how old she was.

Exercise 1

Which sentences are correct?

1 I wanted to know whether there was a post office nearby. ❏

2 Could you tell me how much a ticket to Edinburgh? ❏

3 She asked us why we were late. ❏

4 I wanted to know how long would it take to get to Manchester. ❏ ❏

5 I wondered if the plan would work. ❏ ❏

6 Penny wanted to know when the concert did start. ❏

Exercise 2

Find the wrong or extra word in each sentence.

1 Yolanda wondered if she had time to wash her hair before she would went out.

2 Sergio wanted the sales assistant to tell him what time the shop was closed.

3 He asked me what if I knew where his car keys were.

4 Michelle wondered whether she could to afford the new dress she had seen.

5 Pietro wanted to know how much did the holiday to Majorca cost.

6 She asked to me what I thought about the movie.

Exercise 3

Match the sentence halves.

1 I wanted to know whether I   a whether she had locked the car.

2 She was lost and asked me if   b if I would give him a lift to the hospital.

3 I wondered whether   c I knew where the Lion Hotel was.

4 He wanted to know   d could take my dog on the train.

5 Jacob asked Sue   e wanted to go for a pizza with her.

6 Trina wondered if Tom   f I should take the job.

Exercise 4

Write the missing words in sentence B so that it means the same as sentence A.

1 A 'Why can't you come out tonight?' she asked me.
  B She asked me why I _____ go out that night.

2 A 'Do you know where the file is?' Bernard asked.
  B Bernard wondered where the file _____.

3 A 'Could you tell me what time the office opens?' the man asked.
  B The man _____ to know what time the office opened.

4 A 'Have you any idea how this game works?' Ian asked the sales assistant.
  B Ian asked _____ the sales assistant had any idea how the game worked.

Exercise 5

Decide if the pairs of sentences have the same meaning.

1 **A** 'Could you tell me what time the pool closes?' he asked.
   B He wondered whether they knew if the pool was closing. ❑

2 **A** 'Do you know how to get to the concert hall from here?' she asked.
   B She asked me whether I knew how to get to the concert hall from there. ❑

3 **A** 'Have you any idea how much this dress cost?' she asked.
   B She wondered whether I knew how much her dress had cost. ❑

4 **A** 'Would you mind telling me what time it is?' he asked.
   B He wanted to know what time it was. ❑

5 **A** 'Would you mind not speaking to me like that?' she asked.
   B She asked him whether he wanted to speak to her. ❑

Exercise 6

Choose the correct word or phrase.

1 Carol wanted to know how much the rent **would be / is**.

2 Trevor **wondered / asked** himself where his girlfriend had got to.

3 Zena asked me if I **did see / had seen** her glasses.

4 I wondered whether we **would have / did have** time to take the mountain route.

5 Michael **wondered / wanted** to know if I had booked him a seat.

6 I asked myself whether I **had done / did** the right thing.

Exercise 7

For each sentence, tick the correct ending.

1 He asked lots of questions and wanted to know
   ❑ whether I still lived in Oxford.
   ❑ did I still lived in Oxford.

2 Pablo wondered
   ❑ why Maria tells him about her new job.
   ❑ why Maria hadn't told him about her new job.

3 My mother was very angry,
   ❑ and demanded to know who I had been out with that night.
   ❑ and demanded to know who did I been out with that night.

4 The reporter interviewed me and asked
   ❑ did I seen the robbers entering the bank.
   ❑ whether I had seen the robbers entering the bank.

5 Laura wanted him to tell her
   ❑ how long he'd been planning her birthday party.
   ❑ how long he did plan her birthday party.

7

Modals (1)

Modals for making predictions with certainty

will/shall and be + going to

In this unit you learn how to talk about the future with **will**, **shall** and **going to**.

Shall and will to talk about the future

You cannot talk about the future with as much certainty as you can about the present or the past. You are usually talking about what you think might happen or what you intend to happen. This is why you often use modal verbs. Although most modal verbs can be used to talk about the future, you most often use **will**.

*He **will** not return for many hours.*

To make a question, you put **will** in front of the subject.

*Will **you** be coming in later?*
*When will **I** see them?*

Shall can be used in the same way as **will** above, but is more common in offers and suggestions.

***Shall** I invite Brian and Costa? What do you think?*
***Shall** we go for a walk together?*

Note the following negative short forms:

*I **shan't** let you go.*
***Won't** you change your mind?*

Using will and going to to make predictions

When you are making predictions about the future that are based on general beliefs, opinions or attitudes, you use **will**.

*The weather tomorrow **will** be warm and sunny.*
*I'm sure you'**ll** enjoy your visit to the zoo.*

When you are using facts or events in the present situation as evidence for a prediction, you use **be + going to**.

*It'**s going to** rain. (= I can see black clouds)*
*I'**m going to** be late for the meeting. (= I woke up too late)*

Using will and going to to talk about decisions and intentions

When you are talking about your own intentions, you use either **will** or **going to**. When you are announcing a decision you have just made or are about to make, you use **will**.

I'm tired. I think I'll go to bed.
I'll ring you tonight.
I'm going to stay at home today.

When you are saying what someone else has decided to do, you use **going to**.

They're going to have a party.
She's going to be an actress.

Remember!

You do not normally use **going to** with the verb **go**. You usually just say **I'm going** rather than **I'm going to go.**

A: What **are** you **going to** do this weekend?

B: I'**m going** to the cinema. NOT ~~I'm going to go to the cinema.~~

Exercise 1

Match the sentences with the pictures, as shown.

1 It's going to fall over.

2 It's going to be hot.

3 She's going to win.

4 It's going to snow.

5 She's going to get married.

6 It's going to sink.

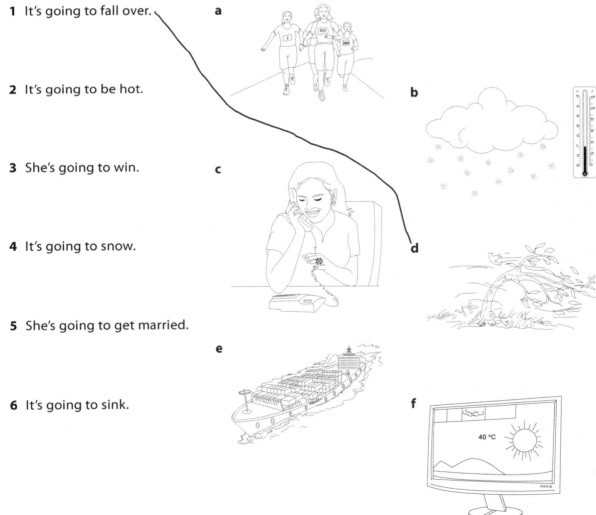

33

Exercise 2

Match the two parts.

1 Look at the crowds arriving at the stadium.
2 The police have stopped that car.
3 Look at the speed that motorcyclist's doing.
4 That little boy has dropped his ice cream.
5 Look at that cat in the garden.
6 Look at the balloons outside that house.

a There are going to be long queues.
b They're going to have a party.
c It's going to go up a tree.
d He's going to have an accident.
e The driver's going to be in trouble.
f He's going to start crying.

Exercise 3

Write the 'going to' form of the verb in brackets to complete each sentence.

1 My brother _____ (climb) Mount Kilimanjaro after his exams.
2 My parents _____ (be) very angry when they see this mess.
3 My friends and I _____ (have) a party at the end of term.
4 The firework display _____ (make) a lot of noise, so I'm staying indoors.
5 I've spent all my money so I _____ (find) a job.
6 I've bought you a present and I know you _____ (love) it.

Exercise 4

Write one missing word in sentence B so that it means the same as sentence A.

1 **A** I'm going to have my hair cut short.
   B I've _____ to have my hair cut short.
2 **A** Shall we do the washing up together?
   B _____ do the washing up together.
3 **A** This is a great film, do you want to watch it with me?
   B This is a great film! _____ you watch it with me?
4 **A** I know the children are tired, but we're nearly home.
   B I know the children are tired, but we _____ soon be home.

Exercise 5

Put each sentence into the correct order.

1 be / when my exams / shall / so happy / I / finish / .

_____

2 wrong / why / you / say / won't / what's / ?

_____

3 after the party / get / how / home / you / will / ?

_____

4 on / probably / my birthday money / some new jeans / I'll / spend / .

_____

5 will / amazed / our news / everyone / be / at / .

_____

6 we'll / you leave / sad / the office / be / when / .

_____

8

Used to

Using *used to* to talk about past situations

`used to + verb`

In this unit you learn how to talk about past situations and habits that are not true any more. You can do this by using the form **used to** and then the verb in the base form.

I used to be overweight, but I've been on a diet. Now I eat healthy food and stay slim.

Read the following dialogue. Two people have just met in the street.

A: *Excuse me. I think I know you. I'm sure I recognize you.*

B: *Oh yes! Me too!* **Did you use to study** *at Liverpool University in the 1990s?*

A: *Yes, I did! Oh, your name is Daisy, isn't it? You* **used to live** *next door to me, if I remember correctly. I'm Anne-Marie.*

B: *Of course, yes, Anne-Marie. I remember now.* **Didn't you use to study** *music? How is that going?*

A: *Oh, I'm afraid I don't play the guitar any more. I work in a bank now. And how about you?*

B: *Well that is strange, because I actually* **used to work** *in a bank but I've just left because I want to become a firefighter!*

Remember!

Used to is a past form. There is no present form. You use **used** in statements, but in the negative and in questions you use **use**.

James **used to have** *long hair but now he's bald.*

He **didn't use to be** *friendly.*

Where **did you use to live**?

35

Exercise 1

Choose the correct word or phrase.

In the area of England just north of Cambridge, called the Fens, the land is below sea level. For many centuries the whole area [1]**used / uses** to flood, but around 300 years ago the land was drained – that is, canals were constructed, so the water went into those instead of covering the fields.

In the nineteenth and early twentieth centuries, the organizations that controlled the canals [2]**used / used to** let water flow into the fields during the winter. When it was cold enough, the water [3]**used to freeze / used to freezing**, and people went skating on the ice. In those days, people living in the Fens [4]**don't use / didn't use** to have much money, and skating was popular because it was free.

My grandmother [5]**uses / used** to live in a village in the Fens. She told me that when she was a child, she [6]**would use / used** to take her skates, a sandwich and an apple, and go skating on the Fens as soon as it was light. And she [7]**didn't use / doesn't use** to go home until it was dark.

Exercise 2

Are the highlighted phrases correct or incorrect in the sentences?

1 My grandparents **didn't use to** ☐ have a fridge.
2 Maria **doesn't use to** ☐ live in Madrid.
3 **Did you use to** ☐ play in the school orchestra?
4 I **use to work** ☐ at the university.
5 **Don't you use to** ☐ play with other children when you were a child?
6 **Have you used to** ☐ be friends with Ralph?

Exercise 3

Complete the sentences by writing one phrase in each gap.

| did you use to like | didn't you use to have | used to look after | |
| didn't you use to go | used to be | didn't use to understand | did Mary use to have |

1 Tell me, _____ to the same school as me?
2 Why _____ spending the whole day on your own?
3 People in this area _____ very poor.
4 I _____ why James Bond films were so popular.
5 Where _____ her dance classes?
6 Who _____ you while your parents were both at work?

Exercise 4

Which sentences are correct?

1 My family hasn't use to go on holidays. ❏
2 The Queen used to have more power than she has today. ❏
3 Does your grandma use to go to the dances in town? ❏
4 Most of the workers use to bring a packed lunch with them. ❏
5 Many children in the village didn't use to have shoes. ❏
6 Did your cousins use to visit you very often? ❏

Exercise 5

Choose the correct word or phrase.

1 The cottage **used to / did used to** have roses growing over its walls.
2 Did your parents **used to / use to** make you go to bed early?
3 Most of the children **use to / used to** go home for lunch.
4 My father **didn't used to / didn't use to** like football.
5 This cupboard **uses to / used to** be used for keeping cleaning materials in.
6 Did this forest **use to / used to** have deer in it?

Exercise 6

Put each sentence into the correct order.

1 didn't / to vote / women / to be allowed / use / .

_____

2 every week / to / used / Gloria / us / visit / .

_____

3 use / like / to / didn't / I / running / .

_____

4 use / live in a flat / didn't / you / to / ?

_____

5 stand on the bridge / to / my brother and I / and wave / used / at the trains / .

_____

6 did / to / get up / you / use / early / ?

_____

9

Modals (2)
Talking about what you can and must do

must, mustn't, need, needn't, don't need, don't have to, have to

In this unit you learn how to use modal verbs and some other expressions to talk about need and obligation.

Must and *have to*

When you want to say it is necessary to do something, you use **must** or **have to**.

> You **must** come to the meeting tomorrow.
> The plants **must** have plenty of sunshine.
> I enjoy parties, unless I **have to** make a speech.
> He **has to** travel to find work.

There is sometimes a difference between **must** and **have to**. When you are stating your own opinion, you normally use **must**.

> I **must** be very careful not to upset him.
> We **must** eat before we go.
> He **must** stop working so hard.

When you are saying what someone else considers to be necessary or where you want to show that something is not your choice, you normally use **have to**.

> They **have to** pay the bill by Thursday.
> She **has to** go now.

Mustn't and *don't have to*

You use **must not** or **mustn't** to say that it is important that something is not done or does not happen.

> You **must not** eat any more sweets.
> They **mustn't** find out that I came here. Keep it secret!

If you **do not have to** do something, it is not necessary for you to do it, but you can do it if you want.

> I **don't have to** finish my homework tonight. The teacher doesn't want it until Tuesday.
> You **don't have to** come if you don't want to.

You only use **must** for obligation and necessity in the present and the future. When you want to talk about the past, you use **had to** rather than **must**.

> Jane **had to** catch the six o'clock train to get back to Norwich in time.
> I **had to** wear a suit.

> ## Remember!
>
> You use **do** when you want to make a question using **have to** and **not have to**.
>
> *How often **do** you have to buy petrol for the car?* not ~~How often have you to buy petrol?~~

Need to and *needn't*

You can also use **need to**.

> *You might **need to** see a doctor.*

You use **needn't** and **don't need to** in a similar way to **don't have to**; to say that it is not necessary to do something.

> *You **don't have to** learn any new computing skills for the job.*
> *You **don't need to** buy anything.*
> *I can pick John up later on tonight. You **needn't** bother.*

You also use **needn't** when you are giving someone permission not to do something.

> *You **needn't** stay any longer tonight.*
> *We **needn't** go to the party if you don't want to.*

Exercise 1

Match the sentence halves.

1 We must set off at once	a before the bank will lend you any money.
2 You don't need to take shampoo –	b to collect his laptop?
3 Does Jim have to go back home	c I understood you the first time.
4 You needn't repeat what you said –	d or we'll miss our flight.
5 I'm afraid you'll have to fill in some forms	e or can you manage by yourself?
6 Do you need any help	f I'm sure the hotel will provide it.

Exercise 2

Which sentences are correct?

1 You mustn't add anything else to the pizza or you'll spoil it. ❏

2 You needn't play your music so loudly or you'll disturb the neighbours. ❏

3 You don't have to come shopping with me if you don't want to. ❏

4 You must call me as soon as you arrive in this country. ❏

5 You need report the burglary to the police. ❏

6 You don't need to be late – you promised you'll arrive on time! ❏

Exercise 3

Choose the correct word or phrase.

1 You **don't have to / mustn't** buy tickets for the concert because it's free.

2 I expect you'll **need to / must** have something to eat before the concert begins.

3 You **need / need to** take some money with you for a programme and refreshments.

4 If you miss the last bus you'll **must / have to** phone me.

5 I **have / must** to get up early in the morning, but I don't mind collecting you.

6 You **must / need** bring home a programme to show me.

Exercise 4

Decide if the pairs of sentences have the same meaning.

1 A I don't need to remind you it's Jack's birthday tomorrow.
  B I mustn't remind you it's Jack's birthday tomorrow. ❑

2 A My children don't have to go to bed until 10 o'clock.
  B My children mustn't go to bed until 10 o'clock. ❑

3 A We needn't ask Oliver to cook dinner tonight.
  B We don't have to ask Oliver to cook dinner tonight. ❑

4 A You needn't let your dog run loose in the park.
  B You mustn't let your dog run loose in the park. ❑

5 A This printer isn't working – we need to replace the ink cartridge.
  B This printer isn't working – we must replace the ink cartridge. ❑

Exercise 5

Complete the sentences by writing one word or phrase in each gap.

| must | don't have | need | mustn't | needs | had to | has to | needn't |

1 You _____ turn on that machine – it isn't safe.

2 It's possible to fly direct to Tokyo – you _____ to stop over in Dubai, unless you really want to.

3 When I was at school I _____ wear school uniform, and I hated it!

4 You've parked your car on double yellow lines, so I'm afraid you _____ pay a parking fine.

5 Laura looks very ill. She _____ to see her doctor.

6 You _____ clean the cooker if you don't want to – I can do it myself.

Exercise 6

Find the wrong or extra word in each sentence.

1 We don't need to any more offers of help.

2 You don't mustn't eat any more chocolates.

3 Trevor has need to be home by 9 o'clock.

4 Sarah didn't must need to do all the cooking herself – I'd offered to help her.

5 You must to have a break before you do any more work.

6 The kitchen does needs to be cleaned thoroughly.

Exercise 7

Are the highlighted words or phrases correct or incorrect in the sentences?

1 You **needn't** ❑ look so sad – I've got some good news for you.
2 Vic cancelled his holiday, but he **didn't need to** ❑.
3 The Government **need** ❑ do more to protect forests.
4 It's very kind of you to give me flowers but you **didn't have to** ❑.
5 It's a secret, so you **needn't** ❑ tell anyone.
6 You **don't must** ❑ hurry – you've got plenty of time.

Exercise 8

Put each sentence into the correct order.

1 late / will / we / hurry / the / so / needn't / be / train / .

_____

2 which / develop / product / decide / company / to / the / has to / .

_____

3 me / you / soon as / arrive / your exam results / must / as / email / .

_____

4 the / more / needs / attract / supporters / team / to / .

_____

5 buy / forget / we / some / mustn't / to / souvenirs / .

_____

6 to / we / so / do / early / have / leave / ?

_____

Exercise 9

Which sentences are correct?

1 If you return the sweater, the shop will have to give you back your money. ❑
2 We don't need to leave yet – it's still too early. ❑
3 You don't have to let me go without giving me the recipe for that delicious cake. ❑
4 I'm very grateful for all you've done, but you needn't go shopping for me as well. ❑
5 Did you must have to go home without seeing the film? ❑
6 You really mustn't keep giving me presents! ❑

10

Modals (3)

Talking about events you are not sure about

must/can't/could/might + be

In this unit you learn how to give your opinion about events. When you are not completely sure about something you need a way to show this. In this unit you learn how to show that you are fairly sure that something is true and also how to show you are not so sure.

Must

When you are fairly sure that something is true, you use **must**. For example:

Marie is on the phone to her friend. They are talking about Marie's new neighbours.

Marie has met the mother of the family, who is called Sylvia Matthews. Marie has not met the rest of Sylvia's family yet, but Sylvia has told her a little bit about her family. While she is talking on the phone, Marie sees a man coming out of the house next door. He is about 45 years old. Marie says to her friend:

   Oh, that **must be** Sylvia's husband. (= Marie is fairly sure that the man is Sylvia's husband)

Can't

When you are fairly sure that something is not true, you use **can't** or **cannot**. For example:

Then Marie sees a different man coming out of the house next door. He is about 25 years old. Sylvia told Marie that her son, Mark, was still at school. Marie says to her friend:

   That **can't be** Sylvia's son. He's too old. (= Marie is fairly sure that the young man is not Sylvia's son)

Could and *might*

When you are not sure whether something is true or not, you use **could** or **might**. For example:

Next, Marie sees the same young man going back into her neighbour's house. Marie knows that Sylvia's daughter Hannah is 22 years old. Marie says to her friend:

*That young man **could be** Hannah's boyfriend. Or he **might be** a friend of Mr Matthews. Or he **could be** a workman doing some work at Sylvia's house. (= Marie is not sure who the man is. She really doesn't know but is guessing.)*

Form	Meaning
Must be	Sure that something is true
Can't be	Sure that something is not true
Could be / might be	Not sure that something is true

Exercise 1

Match the two parts.

1 She left here at 4 o'clock.

2 She's not answering the phone.

3 She looks just like him.

4 I wonder why she's not joining us for dinner at the restaurant tonight.

5 She only looks about 14.

6 She's smiling at us.

a She can't be our new teacher!

b She could be asleep.

c That's good. She can't be too angry with us, then!

d She must be his sister.

e She must be there by now.

f She might not have enough money.

Exercise 2

Choose the correct word.

1 The woman with him is far too young to be his wife. She **can't / must** be his daughter.

2 I'm not sure where Josh is. I'm guessing he **might / must** be at Al's house.

3 You **must / can't** be nice and warm in your thick coat!

4 Sophie **must / can't** be too unhappy if she's laughing.

5 I haven't seen our neighbours for a while. I suppose they **could / can't** be on holiday.

6 Suzie only left half an hour ago. She **can't / might** be back home already!

Exercise 3

Are the highlighted words correct or incorrect in the sentences?

1 Adam's been teaching for over ten years. He **must** ☐ be older than 30.

2 I don't know why she's not at work today. I suppose she **could** ☐ be ill.

3 It's freezing and Eva's not even wearing a coat! She **might** ☐ be so cold.

4 He **must** ☐ be Sophia's dad. He's not old enough!

5 I'm not sure who the guy standing next to Stella is. I guess he **might** ☐ be her boyfriend.

6 That **can't** ☐ be the doctor! She's far too young.

Exercise 4

Put each sentence into the correct order.

1 stuck / he / be / might / traffic / in / .

_____

2 at / must / 30 / be / Sara / least / .

_____

3 suppose he / her / I / be / son / could / .

_____

4 might / sister / she / Maria's / be / .

_____

5 can't / be / he / the driver / car / of / the / .

_____

6 shop / he / of / must / be / the / the owner / .

_____

Exercise 5

Decide if the pairs of sentences have the same meaning.

1 A That little boy must be Rebecca's son. ❑
   B I am sure that little boy is Rebecca's son.

2 A She could still be in bed. ❑
   B She is definitely still in bed.

3 A You must be tired after such a long journey. ❑
   B I am sure you are tired after such a long journey.

4 A Paul might be at work. ❑
   B Paul is possibly at work.

5 A It can't be later than 10 o'clock. ❑
   B It is probably later than 10 o'clock.

Exercise 6

Which sentences are correct?

1 She must to be staying with her mother. ❑
2 Sophia might be away at the moment. ❑
3 She could be Spanish or Italian. ❑
4 Those kids can't to be any older than Anna. ❑
5 You must be so pleased with your exam results! ❑
6 Tom mustn't be too ill if he's eating so well. ❑

11

Showing how certain you are about situations

In this unit you learn more ways to talk about how sure you are about events and situations.

How to talk about how certain you are

How sure are you?

– –	–	+	+ +	+ + +
I'm **not at all** sure	I'm **not** sure	I'm **fairly** sure	I'm sure	I'm **absolutely** sure

A: Oh, there's nobody else here. Are you **sure** the meeting is here?
B: I'm **fairly sure**. It is usually in this room.

How sure are you?

–/+	+	+ +
Might + verb May + verb	—	Going to + verb
—	I believe	I know
—	—	It's obvious It's clear

Might/may and going to

Hello, is that the office? It's Alan here. I've missed my train. I'm afraid I**'m going to be** late for work. I **might be** able to get there for 10 o'clock.

(= Alan is sure he is going to be late for work. He is not sure whether he will get to the office by 10 o'clock or not)

It's clear and it's obvious

It**'s clear** to me that you need to work harder if you want to pass your exams.

I believe and I know

A: Hello, Mr Yakimoto. This is Mr Swift. **I believe** you have met before.
B: Hello, yes we have. I met him in Japan last year, and **I know** he will want to discuss the new project today!

How to talk about your preferences

A: *Would you like to have a pizza with me?*
B: ***I'd prefer not to**. I don't really like pizza. **I prefer** Chinese food.*

A: *Would you like to come out for a drink tonight?*
B: ***I would rather not**. I'm too tired.*

A: ***I'd rather not** go to the cinema tonight. Can we just watch TV?*
B: *OK, but you know **I prefer watching** DVDs. Can we do that instead?*

Exercise 1

Write the missing words in sentence B so that it means the same as sentence A.

1 **A** I think that's Charles on the phone.
   B It _____ be Charles on the phone.

2 **A** I think I'm right. That looks like Mr Johnson talking to my wife.
   B I am _____ sure that is Mr Johnson talking to my wife.

3 **A** I would rather eat fish than chicken.
   B I _____ eating fish to chicken.

4 **A** I don't think that bird is a magpie; it's too big.
   B I'm _____ sure if that bird is a magpie; it's too big.

Exercise 2

Are the highlighted words correct or incorrect in the sentences?

1 That **could** ❑ be the postman. He usually comes around this time in the morning.

2 Look at those clouds. It **must** ❑ rain tonight.

3 I haven't decided where to go on holiday. I **may** ❑ go to France because I love French food.

4 I **might** ❑ come and see you tomorrow, if I finish my work early.

5 I would rather **having** ❑ a pizza tonight.

6 Be careful of that dog. It might **to** ❑ jump.

Exercise 3

Choose the correct word or phrase.

1 I **would rather / prefer** not eat too much, as I'm on a diet.

2 I'm not at all **obvious / sure** that I closed all the windows.

3 Jack's so tired I **know / would rather** he'll sleep well tonight.

4 Jenny would like to go out this evening, but her husband would **prefer / rather** to stay at home.

5 It's **absolutely / obvious** that Malcolm is going to win.

6 Would you like a chocolate, or would you **prefer / rather** have an ice cream?

Exercise 4

Find the wrong or extra word in each sentence.

1 I am fairly not sure I had £10 in my purse. I wonder where I spent it.

2 I think it's going in to snow; it's getting colder and colder.

3 I will buy those shoes after all. I am absolutely sure about they will look great with my blue dress.

4 What would you prefer to doing tonight? Shall we go to the cinema or stay at home and watch TV?

5 I think I would quite like to learn how to make my own clothes, so I may to do a course at the college.

6 I would rather not to come to the shopping mall with you; it will be so busy on a Saturday.

Exercise 5

Decide if the pairs of sentences have the same meaning.

1 **A** I think I know that woman.
  B I may know that woman. ❑

2 **A** Watch out! That bottle is going to fall!
  B Watch out! I am sure that bottle will fall. ❑

3 **A** I know I put my glasses on the table, but they are not there now.
  B I may have put my glasses on the table, but they are not there now. ❑

4 **A** Wait for a few minutes; the soup might be too hot to eat.
  B Wait for a few minutes; I know the soup isn't cool enough to eat. ❑

5 **A** Angela, this is Simon Woods. I believe you are both studying history at university.
  B Angela, this is Simon Woods. You might both be studying history at university. ❑

Exercise 6

Which sentences are correct?

1 I would rather not listen to classical music if you don't mind, Bob. I prefer jazz. ❑

2 I don't like the country. I prefer to living in a city. ❑

3 I would prefer to work closer to home but there are no jobs in my town. ❑

4 What would you rather to have, tea of coffee? ❑

5 I prefer taking my time when I write long letters to people. It helps me think about everything I want to say. ❑

6 I'd prefer for not to have a break right now. I need to finish this job first. ❑

Exercise 7

Put each sentence into the correct order.

1 I / always / right / believe / I'm / !

_____

2 Jenny / after / all that / may / practice / win / the competition / .

_____

3 It's / some / homework / clear / help / you / with your / need / .

_____

4 I'm / last Christmas / this book / absolutely / you / I gave / sure / .

_____

5 than / I / rather / would / get / walk / a taxi / .

_____

6 what / fish / would / chicken or / for dinner, / you / prefer / ?

_____

Exercise 8

Match the questions to the answers.

1 May I smoke?

2 What do you think? Do I need a new car?

3 Shall we catch the 7.30 a.m. train tomorrow?

4 Which do you like better, the green dress or the red one?

5 Would you like to sit down while you are waiting?

6 Are you a vegetarian?

a You don't need one. I'd prefer you not to spend that much money.

b I'd rather you didn't.

c No, but I prefer vegetables to meat dishes.

d I'd prefer a later one if you don't mind.

e I prefer the blue one actually.

f I'd rather stand if that's OK.

Exercise 9

Put the correct word in each gap.

| prefer | absolutely | not | rather | know | may | going |

Dear Margaret

I am sorry I can't come to your birthday party, but I [1]_____ you will like the present I bought for you. You always talk about learning to ride a bicycle, and I finally decided to buy you a new bike. I'm [2]_____ sure you will like the colour. It's red, your favourite. It's [3]_____ to be great because we can cycle everywhere and get fit at the same time. You [4]_____ need some cycling lessons though, and I think the local school is running courses next month. Why don't you give them a ring and find out?

I would [5]_____ bring the bike to your house this weekend. Will you be at home? Give me a ring and let me know what time you would [6]_____.

Happy birthday!

Sharon

12

Second and third conditionals

Second conditional: *If* + past simple + *would* + present simple

Third conditional: *If* + past perfect + *would have* + past participle

In this unit you learn how to talk about situations that are not real. Sometimes you want to talk about things that are unlikely to happen or things that could have happened but did not.

If you won a million pounds, what would you do?
We asked some young people in London.

Tariq (18)
I'd buy a house for my parents.

Lucy (16)
I'd travel the world! I'd go to Australia and Thailand.

Ally (21)
I'd stop working in the factory and I'd become an artist.

Kev (23)
I'd ask my girlfriend to marry me.

Using the second conditional

Winning a million pounds is unusual! The young people above have been asked to imagine winning that much money. Because they do not think the situation is going to happen they use conditional forms.

There are two parts to the form: one part contains the past simple (**If you won**) and the second part contains **would** (**what would you do?**).

*If I **had** enough money, I **would buy** the car.*
*If he **was coming**, he **would ring**.*

> *Remember!*
>
> You do not normally use **would** in both parts of the sentence. You do not say *If I would do it, I would do it like this.*

Using the third conditional

When you are talking about something that could have happened in the past but did not happen, you use the past perfect in the conditional clause. In the main clause, you use **would have** and **-ed**.

> If he **had realized** that, he **would have run** away.
> If I **had won** the competition, I **would have been** more famous now.

Unless

You can also use a conditional clause beginning with **unless**.

> You **wouldn't have passed** your exams **unless you had worked** as hard as you did.

Note that you can often use **if . . . not** instead of **unless**.

> You **would have failed** your exams **if you had not worked** as hard as you did.

Exercise 1

Match the sentence halves.

1	If we spent more time relaxing,	**a**	we'd feel less stressed.
2	We would have got up on time this morning	**b**	if we exercised more.
3	If we didn't go on holiday every year,	**c**	if we hadn't borrowed money from the bank.
4	We would all be much healthier	**d**	we'd have had more time to have fun.
5	If we hadn't spent so long doing homework,	**e**	if we'd gone to bed earlier last night.
6	We wouldn't have been able to buy the flat	**f**	we'd save more money.

Exercise 2

Are the highlighted words correct or incorrect in this text?

Damien's bad day

Damien had had a bad day and he only had himself to blame. That morning, he had been over an hour late for work. The reason? He had forgotten to set his alarm. If the sound of the children going to school **hadn't** ❏ woken him up, he would **have** ❏ probably never have got to work at all.

Then there had been that misunderstanding at work. Why on earth, he thought for the hundredth time, hadn't he checked the list of people he was sending the invitation to his birthday party to? If he had **have** ❏, he would have realized that he'd **forgot** ❏ to include his boss. 'No chance of a promotion now,' he thought gloomily.

After that, the day had gone from bad to worse. He would never **argued** ❏ with a parking attendant again, he resolved. His fine had been doubled because of his 'insolent attitude'. Mind you, if Damien **had** ❏ remembered to buy a ticket, the whole unpleasant episode wouldn't have happened in the first place. 'Yes,' Damien concluded, 'I have had better days.'

Exercise 3

Put each sentence into the correct order.

1 sunbathe / unless / a lot of suntan lotion. / I wouldn't / I wore / in the hot sun

_____

2 studied so hard, / if Marco / he wouldn't / in the exam / have got such good grades / hadn't / .

_____

3 would / I / you'd like to / accept the job, / be delighted to hire you. / if

_____

4 if / worked at the same company. / have / they hadn't / Laura wouldn't / met Andy

_____

5 if London / poor parts of the city / hadn't / have been rebuilt. / wouldn't / won the 2012 Olympic bid,

_____

6 would go / if Sue / they / let someone look after the dog. / abroad more on holiday / would

_____

Exercise 4

Decide if the pairs of sentences have the same meaning.

1 A I wouldn't play the lottery unless there was a good chance that I'd win.
  B If there was a better chance of winning, I'd play the lottery. ☐

2 A Maria wouldn't have crashed the car if she hadn't been so tired.
  B If she had had more sleep, Maria would have crashed the car. ☐

3 A If you would feed my cat while I'm away, I'd be very grateful.
  B If you had fed my cat while I was away, I'd have been very grateful. ☐

4 A Would you have been happier if you hadn't had to work?
  B Would you be happier if you didn't have to work? ☐

5 A Mohammed wouldn't have attended an American university if his teacher hadn't recommended it.
  B If his teacher had recommended it, Mohammed would have gone to an American university. ☐

Exercise 5

Choose the correct word or phrase.

1 If the sun **hadn't / had / wouldn't have** shone, the picnic would have been a disaster.

2 Paul **had / would have / wouldn't have** got to work on time if the traffic hadn't been so heavy.

3 I wouldn't enter a competition unless there was a good chance that I **wouldn't win / win / would win**.

4 If Francesca **wants / had wanted / wanted** a new motorbike, her parents would buy one for her.

5 There **wouldn't be / would be / wouldn't have been** so much rubbish if we recycled more.

Exercise 6

Find the wrong or extra word in each sentence.

1 If Michelangelo hadn't painted the Sistine Chapel, he wouldn't have had become one of the most famous artists of all time.

2 If you had had the money, would you buy a house abroad?

3 If Tim would got the professional position he applied for, we'd all miss him.

4 There would have be less crime if unemployment wasn't so high.

5 I wouldn't have asked her out unless you had not told me that it was OK.

6 Gemma wouldn't be so fit if she didn't have had a personal trainer.

Exercise 7

Which sentences are correct?

1 They wouldn't have cancelled the rock concert unless they had had to. ❑

2 He wouldn't have applied for the job if you hadn't have suggested it. ❑

3 Pollution would be reduced if everyone was used the bus. ❑

4 Unless we didn't walk the dog twice a day, he would get fat. ❑

5 The Olympic ceremony wouldn't have been so enjoyable if it had rained. ❑

6 The student would have raised his hand if he had known the answer. ❑

Exercise 8

Complete the text by writing one word in each gap.

Matteo: If I ¹_____ you whether you believed in coincidences, Dao-Ming, what ²_____ you say?

Dao-Ming: What a strange question! Let me see, I think I ³_____ probably say that sometimes amazing things happen which are difficult to explain, ⁴_____ you used the word 'coincidence'. Like that time I was looking for a copy of my favourite book from when I was a child in a second-hand book store. I eventually found a copy, opened the front cover and there was my name written on the first page: Dao-Ming, 1985.

Matteo: Amazing! So what you're saying is, if you ⁵_____ visited that book store at that time, you ⁶_____ never have found that particular book? I can sort of believe that that's a coincidence, but how about those urban myths where the same unlikely event happens twice? Like that story of a man who caught the same baby falling from a window twice, on two separate occasions.

Dao-Ming: Gosh, if he ⁷_____ been in the right place at the right time, the baby ⁸_____ have survived.

Matteo: That's right, but don't you think it's a bit of a tall story? I mean, one careless mistake is believable, but if I ⁹_____ the baby's mother, I ¹⁰_____ ever let the child go near an open window again. ¹¹_____ you?

13

Conditionals

as if, as though, as long as, provided, provided that

In this unit you revise the conditional forms, and you learn some other ways to talk about situations that are not real.

Using conditional forms

Form	Conditional clause	Main clause	Meaning
First conditional	If I **do** more sports	**I'll be** fitter	This is possible. I want to be fitter so I might start to do more sports.
Second conditional	If I **did** more sports	**I'd be** fitter	This is not likely. Perhaps I want to be fitter but I am probably not going to do more sports as I don't have enough time
Third conditional	If I **had done** more sports	**I'd have been** fitter	When I was younger I did not do a lot of sports and I was not very fit

As if and *as though*

When you want to say that something might not be true, or is definitely not true, you use **as if** or **as though**.

> Asha: *Melanie reacted **as if** she didn't know about the race. (= Asha thinks that Melanie did know about the race)*
> Peter: *Tina acts **as though** she owns the place. (= Peter thinks that Tina does not own the place)*

After **as if** or **as though**, you often use a past simple form even when you are talking about the present. This helps to show that the information is not true.

> *Presidents can't dispose of companies **as if** people **didn't** exist.*
> *She looks after him **as though** he **was** her own son.*

You can also use **as if** or **as though** to say how someone or something feels, looks or sounds.

> *He looked **as if** he hadn't slept very much.*
> *Mary sounded **as though** she had just run all the way.*

Other ways of beginning conditional clauses

You can also use **as long as**, **provided**, **provided that**, **providing**, **providing that** or **so long as**. These expressions are all used to show that one thing only happens or is true if another thing happens or is true.

> *We were all right **as long as** we kept quiet.*
> *She was prepared to come, **provided that** she could bring her daughter.*
> *The system works well **providing that** you remember to take your passport with you.*

Exercise 1

For each question, tick the correct answer.

1 I'll help you peel the vegetables, on condition that you
- ❏ will you look after the kids tomorrow?
- ❏ looked after the kids tomorrow.
- ❏ look after the kids tomorrow.

2 Supposing Mike gets good grades this year,
- ❏ will he go to university?
- ❏ would he go to university?
- ❏ would he have gone to university?

3 Charlie ate the roast chicken as if
- ❏ she hadn't eaten in weeks.
- ❏ she didn't eat in weeks.
- ❏ she wouldn't have eaten in weeks.

4 Providing that you finish your household chores on time,
- ❏ I'd let you go out tonight.
- ❏ I'd have let you go out tonight.
- ❏ I'll let you go out tonight.

5 I'd go to the USA on holiday, providing
- ❏ I had enough money for the plane ticket.
- ❏ I didn't have enough money for the plane ticket.
- ❏ I have enough money for the plane ticket.

Exercise 2

Choose the correct word or phrase.

Sue: Gary, can I try out this quiz on you? It's called 'How honest are you?' If you [1]**will answer / answer / answered** all the questions truthfully, I'll buy you lunch.

Gary: Well, OK, providing you [2]**don't / won't / wouldn't** judge me on my answers.

Sue: Don't be silly. Right, the first question is: Supposing you [3]**find / found / would find** some money in the street, [4]**would you / will you / would you have** take it to the police?

Gary: Of course I [5]**won't / wouldn't have / wouldn't**. How [6]**will the police know / would the police know / had the police known** who lost the money in the first place?

Sue: Fair point, I suppose, but what if the money you found [7]**would be / was / is** inside a wallet? You know, along with things like identity cards and credit cards?

Gary: Well, that's easy, isn't it? I [8]**will / would have / would** definitely take it to the police then.

Exercise 3

Put the correct word in each gap.

| if | provided | had | as | supposing | couldn't | have | condition | long | hadn't |

Dear Alessandra

I hope you're well. I'm OK, but I had a nasty shock the other day. I got knocked off my bike by a car! Don't worry, I wasn't badly hurt. It could [1]_____ been much worse if I [2]_____ been so lucky.

Here's what happened: I was riding towards the botanical gardens, when I heard a car coming up behind me. It sounded as [3]_____ the driver was in a hurry. The car's engine was roaring and the car was very close to me.

Suddenly, I felt the car pull out next to me [4]_____ though it was trying to overtake. At the same time, I saw a bus coming the other way fast. I thought the car and the bus were going to hit each another. The driver obviously thought the same, as he slowed down and moved in, behind my bike again. But as he was doing so, he hit my back wheel.

I flew off my bike and landed on the grass next to the road. I was wearing a thick jacket and a helmet, which protected my head, but [5]_____ I hadn't been? I don't like to think about it. Unfortunately, I did land hard on my wrist and heard it snap. The hospital told me it was a bad break and put it in plaster.

The nice doctor who treated my arm said that [6]_____ I don't use my hand for six weeks, my wrist will be as good as new. I'm so glad it was my left wrist that broke as if it [7]_____ been my right, I [8]_____ have written you this letter! One good piece of news is that my father has decided that cycling is dangerous. He said that as [9]_____ as I study hard this year, he'll buy me a car after my exams! Result!

So you see, it all turned out OK in the end! How about you? Please write and tell me all your news.

Take care

Love

Mariana

x

Exercise 4

Put each sentence into the correct order.

1 that / travel outside rush hour / , public transport won't be too busy / providing / you / .

_____

2 Abdul had / felt, she / have gone away / if / wouldn't / told Leyla how he / .

_____

3 be reduced / we stop using / so much energy. / global warming / as long as / will

_____

4 it was / every day, / people miss rain / supposing / would / sunny / ?

_____

5 didn't / the tourist industry / if Britain / would suffer / have a monarchy, / .

_____

6 as you / kindly, / they will treat you / treat people / the same way / as long / .

_____

Exercise 5

Are the highlighted words correct or incorrect in this text?

Supposed ❑ you needed a new car, but didn't know what you wanted? That's where Cleys of Hertfordshire can help.

We have a range of models by different manufacturers for you to choose from. **Provided** ❑ that you bring your driver's licence along with you, you can test drive any car you like.

We have a staff of knowledgeable salespeople who can help you make the best selection to suit your lifestyle. For instance, if you **would** ❑ have a family, they'll show you stylish hatchbacks with plenty of room for children and all their belongings.

There are cars in our showroom to suit a range of budgets. We offer competitive monthly rates, as long **as** ❑ you have a guaranteed monthly income and a clear credit rating.

Cleys is so customer-centred that we'll even allow you to take any car you like home for a few days for a long-term test drive and we won't charge you a penny, **in** ❑ condition that it's returned clean and without bumps or scratches. Now, we can't say fairer than that, can we?

If it looks as **through** ❑ a new car is just out of your budget, our sales team will do their best to track you down a used car instead. We only source these from approved dealers and offer a five-year warranty, so you'll have the peace of mind that the car will last you for years to come.

We'll even offer you your money back on a new car that you've bought, if you **aren't** ❑ completely satisfied with it after a few weeks. So what are you waiting for? Come and see Cleys of Hertfordshire today.

Exercise 6

Which sentences are correct?

1 Providing you saw a famous person, would you ask for their autograph? ❏

2 I'll lend you the funds you need, as long you promise to pay me back. ❏

3 Brian's new hairstyle is awful. It looks as though he cut it himself! ❏

4 If Steph had remembered to take her swimsuit on holiday to Turkey,
   she wouldn't buy one while she was there. ❏

5 Would you buy a new bicycle, supposed you could afford one? ❏

6 Provided you eat a balanced diet, you won't put on any weight. ❏

Exercise 7

Decide if the pairs of sentences have the same meaning.

1 **A** Provided you work late tonight, you can have the day off tomorrow.
  B I'll let you have the day off tomorrow, as long as you work late tonight. ❏

2 **A** If you hadn't lent him the cash, he wouldn't have bought those expensive trainers.
  B Supposing you had lent him the cash, he would have bought those expensive trainers. ❏

3 **A** The little boy was pale and shook all over. He looked as though he'd seen a ghost.
  B It was as if the little boy had seen a ghost; he was pale and shook all over. ❏

4 **A** Ennis ran the 10,000 metres as if her life depended on it.
  B If her life had depended on it, Ennis would have run. ❏

5 **A** If you come shoe shopping with me, I'll go to the football match tomorrow.
  B I'll go shoe shopping on condition that you go to the football match tomorrow. ❏

Exercise 8

Write the missing words in sentence B so that it means the same as sentence A.

1 **A** I'll mow the lawn on condition that you do the dishes.
  B _____ as you do the dishes, I'll mow the lawn.

2 **A** If you could travel to any planet in the solar system, which would you go to?
  B _____ you could travel to any planet, which would you go to?

3 **A** If you buy a sofa now, you can pay for it over 12 months, interest-free!
  B On _____ you buy a sofa now, you can pay for it over 12 months, interest-free.

4 **A** If we had gone to Malaysia in November, it would have been even hotter.
  B _____ we had gone to Malaysia in November, it would have been even hotter.

14

Present simple and present perfect in future time

Using present verbs to talk about the future

In this unit you learn some more ways to talk about the future.

Boy	Can we go to visit Granny today?
Mum	Yes. **As soon as I get** home from work, **we'll go** to the shops. **After we've been** to the shops, **we'll go** to visit Granny.

What are the boy and his mother doing first? They are going shopping.

Present simple

When you use **if** and time clauses beginning with words such as **when** or **until**, you normally use the present simple to talk about the future.

I do / work / like, etc.

> *If he **comes**, I'll let you know.*
> *Please start when you **are** ready.*
> *We won't start the meeting until everyone **arrives**.*

Present perfect

If you want to show that one thing has to happen before another thing can be done, you can use the present perfect for future events. You use words like **until**, **when** and **as soon as** to show when this will happen. The present perfect is formed by using the present simple of **have** and the **-ed** participle of the main verb.

> *We won't start until everyone **has arrived**.*
> *I'll let you know when I **have arranged** everything.*
> *She can have the toy back when she **has stopped** crying.*
> *I'll write to you as soon as I **have heard** from Jenny.*

Will or can	Adverbial	Present perfect
We won't start	until	everyone has arrived.
I'll let you know	when	I have arranged everything.
She can have the toy back	when	she has stopped crying.

Exercise 1

Which sentences are correct?

1 It'll be dark when you finish sports practice. ❑

2 Could you call me when you've decided what size you need? ❑

3 Shall we go to the swimming pool before it'll get too crowded? ❑

4 Can I borrow that novel when you've finished reading it, please? ❑

5 As soon as the play will end, we'll have to leave. ❑

6 I'll go to the hairdresser while you have your nails done. ❑

Exercise 2

Match the sentence halves.

1 The children have decided to go to the park

2 Shall we go trekking in the mountains

3 Remind me to give you my email address

4 John wants to spend six months travelling round the world

5 The shop will have lots of new products

6 Will you water my plants

a as soon as the sun comes out.

b as soon as the sale has finished.

c before the weather gets too cold?

d before you go home.

e when he graduates from university.

f while I'm on holiday?

Exercise 3

Are the highlighted words correct or incorrect in the sentences?

1 I'd like to take you to visit my grandmother before you **leave** ❑ this country.

2 As soon as John has **checked** ❑ his emails we can go to the flea market.

3 When Cathy **will arrive** ❑ , we'll start singing 'Happy birthday'.

4 I don't expect many people in the audience will stay until the concert **will end** ❑.

5 Sharif is going to play football after he **has had** ❑ something to eat.

6 We're not leaving until Mike **has apologized** ❑ to his grandfather.

Exercise 4

Complete the sentences by writing one word or phrase in each gap.

| will be | has left | has been | has seen | will leave | leave | is | will see |

1 I hope your son will visit us while he _____ in Australia.

2 It _____ nearly midnight before we arrive.

3 As soon as Penny _____, we can do the washing up.

4 Billy hopes he _____ the Taj Mahal while he's in India.

5 Amina is going to tell me what she thinks of the film, as soon as she _____ it.

6 If we're not careful, the train _____ before we reach the station.

Exercise 5

Find the words or phrases that do not belong.

1 **Let's go home as soon as the film ....**
ends
will end
has ended

2 **Do you think it .... sunny tomorrow?**
is going to be
will be
is

3 **Will you go to dental school when you .... high school?**
will leave
leave
have left

4 **We'll contact you as soon as we .... our decision.**
have made
make
will make

5 **Please phone us when you .... your hotel.**
reach
will reach
have reached

6 **I'm sure the limousine .... soon.**
arrives
is going to arrive
will arrive

7 **We'll have a big lunch when you .... your work.**
have finished
finish
will finish

8 **Brian says he .... for an hour every day in future.**
is going to cycle
cycles
will cycle

Exercise 6

Choose the correct word or phrase.

1 Dinner will be cold by the time the children **have washed / will wash** their hands.

2 I'm sure we **will enjoy / enjoy** ourselves next weekend when we go to the seaside.

3 The builders are going to do some work on my house while I **am / will be** in hospital.

4 By the time Mandy **will arrive / arrives** I'll be really hungry.

5 When the advertisement appears in tomorrow's newspaper, I'm sure a lot of people **apply / will apply** for the job.

6 After you **have repaired / will repair** your bike, could you fix mine too, please?

15

Adverbs

Words that add information about when, how often and how things happen

still, yet, any longer, any more, even, only

In this unit you learn to talk about when things happen and for how long they continue. You also learn some words to talk about how things happen.

Using different time adverbs

You use time adverbs (or adverbials of duration) to say that an event or situation is continuing, stopping or is not happening at the moment.

Still

You use **still** to say that a situation continues to be true. You can put **still** in front of the main verb.

> *My family **still** lives in India.*
> *You will **still** get tickets, if you hurry.*

You can put **still** after **be** as a main verb.

> *Martin's mother died, but his father is **still** alive.*

You can use **still** after the subject and before the verb phrase in negative sentences to express surprise or impatience.

> *You **still** haven't given us the keys.*
> *It was after midnight, and he **still** wouldn't leave.*

Yet

You use **yet** at the end of negative sentences and questions to say that something has not happened, but is expected to happen later.

> *We haven't got the tickets **yet**.*
> *Have you joined the swimming club **yet**?*

> ## Remember!
> Notice how you can use **still** and **yet** with the same meaning:
> *I **still** haven't met my girlfriend's parents.*
> *I haven't met my girlfriend's parents **yet**.*

Any longer and any more

You use **any longer** and **any more** at the end of negative clauses to say that a past situation has ended.

> *I wanted the job, but I couldn't wait **any longer**.*
> *He's not going to play **any more**.*

Even

You use **even** to show that what you are saying is surprising. You put **even** in front of the surprising part of your statement.

> ***Even** Anthony enjoyed it.*
> *She liked him **even** when she was arguing with him.*
> *You didn't **even** enjoy it very much.*

Only

Only is used to say that something is the one thing that happens.

> *There is **only** one train that goes from Denmark to Sweden by night.*
> *I **only** see my brother at weekends.*
> *New technology will **only** be introduced if the workers agree to it.*

Exercise 1

Choose the correct word or phrase.

1 I bought this watch ten years ago and I **yet / still / even** wear it every day.

2 You can have this camera if you like, because I don't use it **any more / still / even**.

3 I called a taxi 20 minutes ago and it **only / still / even** hasn't arrived.

4 Have you found out what happened to your luggage any **more / any longer / yet**?

5 I didn't mean to be rude; I was **only / still / even** trying to explain the problem.

Exercise 2

Decide if the pairs of sentences have the same meaning.

1 **A** I can't wear these jeans any more, as they don't fit properly.
   B I can't wear these jeans any longer, as they don't fit properly. ☐

2 **A** These films are only suitable for children under the age of ten.
   B Only these films are suitable for children under the age of ten. ☐

3 **A** I still haven't met any of your new friends from university.
   B I haven't met any of your new friends from university yet. ☐

4 **A** We haven't told anyone about our plans, except our parents.
   B We haven't told anyone about our plans, even our parents. ☐

Exercise 3

Put the correct word or phrase in each gap.

| yet | ever | any more | even | only | still | no longer |

Hi Dad

How are you and Mum? I can go online now, so here's our news.

When we came to look round our new flat, we met the neighbours downstairs. I thought then they were rather unfriendly, but I don't think that [1]_____. They [2]_____ helped us carry all our boxes up to the flat. However, you won't be surprised to hear that we [3]_____ haven't unpacked them all!

We haven't met the neighbours upstairs [4]_____, but we've [5]_____ been here two weeks and they were away when we arrived.

Anyway, although I wasn't sure if I'd like this place before we moved, I'm [6]_____ worried. I'm sure everything will be just fine.

See you soon

Mike

Exercise 4

Put each sentence into the correct order.

1 because the film / so boring / walked out. / was / even / some people

_____

2 I applied for / still / the job / waiting to hear / I'm / about / .

_____

3 I don't / any more / I've / to play volleyball / want / decided / .

_____

4 the children / to bed / gone / yet / why / haven't / ?

_____

5 the sports centre / allowed / with a coach / into / were only / students / .

_____

6 catch / stay any longer / because / our bus / we had to / we couldn't / .

_____

Exercise 5

Which sentences are correct?

1 I wasn't busy, only I was watching television. ❑

2 Will you still need this computer when you get your new laptop? ❑

3 This jacket doesn't fit me any more, so I'll have to get a new one. ❑

4 I put the dishes in the dishwasher, but it yet hasn't finished the cycle yet. ❑

5 I can no longer believe anything that man says. ❑

6 Even she didn't wait to hear my explanation, she just walked out. ❑

Exercise 6

Are the highlighted words or phrases correct or incorrect in the sentences?

1 We're **yet** ❑ not sure if we can borrow my brother's car tonight.

2 **Even** ❑ I phoned the school, but no one knows where Kevin is.

3 Josh isn't at home **any longer** ❑ ; he's at university in the States.

4 Stella told Cora that she didn't want **any more** ❑ to work with her, because she was lazy.

5 I haven't decided what to do when I leave the army. I'm **still** ❑ trying to make up my mind.

6 I didn't mean to annoy you. I **only** ❑ asked if you were busy.

Exercise 7

For each sentence, tick the correct ending.

1 I asked her again and again
   ❑ but she even wouldn't tell me where she'd been.
   ❑ but she still wouldn't tell me where she'd been.
   ❑ but she yet wouldn't tell me where she'd been.

2 We've been working on it for over two years now
   ❑ and it even isn't finished.
   ❑ and it isn't finished any more.
   ❑ and it still isn't finished.

3 Klaus and Amanda are getting married next year,
   ❑ but they haven't set a date for their wedding yet.
   ❑ but they haven't set a date for their wedding still.
   ❑ but they haven't set a date for their wedding any longer.

4 We are definitely going ahead with the sale, but
   ❑ we yet haven't agreed the terms of the contract.
   ❑ we still haven't agreed the terms of the contract.
   ❑ we even haven't agreed the terms of the contract.

5 Has Sita
   ❑ had her baby still?
   ❑ had her baby any longer?
   ❑ had her baby yet?

6 Years had passed and
   ❑ they were yet paying off their debts.
   ❑ they were even paying off their debts.
   ❑ they were still paying off their debts.

16

Asking for, giving and refusing permission

can, could, may

In this unit you learn different ways of asking whether you can do something, and how to tell someone that they can or can't do something.

Can, could and *may*

Giving permission

When you want to give someone permission to do something, you use **can**.

> *You **can** borrow that pen if you want to.*
> *She **can** go with you.*

May is also used to give permission, but this is more formal.

> *You **may** leave as soon as you have finished.*

Asking for permission

When you are asking for permission to do something, you use **can** or **could**. If you ask in a very simple and direct way, you use **can**.

> ***Can** I ask a question?*
> ***Can** we have something to wipe our hands on, please?*

Could is more polite than **can**.

> ***Could** I just interrupt a minute?*

May is also used to ask permission, but this is more formal.

> ***May** I sit here?*

Refusing permission

When you want to refuse someone permission to do something, you use **cannot** and **can't**.

> *Boy: Mum. Can I have some sweets?*
> *Mum: No, you **can't**!*

> ### *Remember!*
>
> **Might** is rather old-fashioned and is not often used in modern English in this way.
>
> ***Might** I inquire if you are the owner?*

Other ways of talking about permission

Questions		Answers
Am I allowed Are we allowed Is it OK	to eat here? to smoke here? to park here? to sit here?	I'm afraid not. Sure, go ahead. Yes, that's fine. Please do.
Is it all right if I Is it all right if we	eat here? smoke here? park here? sit here?	
Would you mind	helping me? holding this? opening the door?	No, not at all! I'm sorry I can't.
Would you mind if	I parked here? I sat here? I ate here? I smoked here?	No, not at all! I'm sorry but you can't. I'm afraid I **do** mind!

Remember!

No, not at all! looks like a negative thing to say but actually when you say it you are saying **Yes, I will help you!**

A: *Would you mind opening the door for me? My hands are full.*

B: *No, not at all!*

A: *Thank you. That was really helpful.*

Exercise 1

Write the missing words in sentence B so that it means the same as sentence A.

1 A Can I take photos in here?

   B Is it _____ if I take photos in here?

2 A You're not really supposed to picnic on the grass.

   B We'd _____ you didn't picnic on the grass.

3 A May I close the front door?

   B Would you _____ if I closed the front door?

4 A Video cameras aren't permitted in here.

   B I'm _____ you're not permitted to use video cameras in here.

5 A You can leave now, if you want.

   B It's fine _____ you to leave now.

6 A Is it OK if I lock my bike up here?

   B Am I allowed _____ lock my bike up here?

Exercise 2

For each question, tick the most polite answer.

1 Excuse me. Can I sit here?
   ❏ Yes, of course.
   ❏ That's fine.

2 Is it OK if I open the door to the balcony?
   ❏ It's OK.
   ❏ Sure. Please do.

3 Is it all right if I change my shoes in here?
   ❏ It's not all right.
   ❏ I'd rather you didn't.

4 May I take the day off tomorrow?
   ❏ I'm afraid that's not possible.
   ❏ You may not.

5 Would you mind if I borrowed your umbrella?
   ❏ No, not at all.
   ❏ No, I wouldn't.

6 Am I allowed to park the truck here?
   ❏ Yes, you are.
   ❏ Yes, go ahead.

Exercise 3

Choose the correct word or phrase.

1 **Is it / Are you** OK if I borrow this textbook?
2 **Are / Would** you mind if I called you later this evening?
3 **May / Would** I sit here?
4 **Is there / Are we** allowed to walk on the grass?
5 **Do you / Could you** tell me the time, please?
6 **Do we / Is it** OK to drink the water from the fountain?

Exercise 4

Put the correct word in each gap.

is | could | mind | afraid | would | course

Hi Jack

Thanks for inviting me to stay at the weekend – it's really kind of you. I've got a couple of favours to ask. First of all, ¹_____ it be OK if I brought my dog? And ²_____ it possible for you to collect us from the station? Also, ³_____ we visit that lovely castle near you while we're there? Thanks! Now to answer your questions: Of ⁴_____ you can borrow my camera for your holiday; I don't ⁵_____ at all. I'll bring it with me. But I'm ⁶_____ I can't bring the stand, as I've lent it to my brother. I hope that's OK. See you soon!

Exercise 5

Which sentences are correct?

1 Are we allowed to use mobiles in here? ❏
2 Would you be mind if I closed the door? ❏
3 Can I to go in here? ❏
4 Would it be all right if I used your scanner? ❏
5 Is it OK we use the visitor's parking? ❏
6 May I come in, please? ❏

Exercise 6

Put each sentence into the correct order.

1 you / would / mind / if / opened / I / gate / the / ?

_____

2 leave / I / may / the / room / ?

_____

3 you / helping / would / me / mind / ?

_____

4 it / OK / is / I / if / wait / outside / ?

_____

5 I / have / could / at / look / a / photos / your / ?

_____

6 borrow / I / can / mobile / your / ?

_____

Exercise 7

Choose the correct word.

1 **A** Can I borrow your pen?
  B I'd rather you **not / didn't**, if you don't mind.

2 **A** May I have a drink, please?
  B Yes, of **sure / course**. Help yourself.

3 **A** Would you mind if I used your desk?
  B No, **not / never** at all.

4 **A** Am I allowed to borrow this bicycle helmet?
  B I'm **sorry / afraid** not.

5 **A** Could I ask you something?
  B Sure, **get / go** ahead.

6 **A** May I leave now?
  B Yes, that's **good / fine**.

Exercise 8

Match the questions to the answers.

1 Would you mind if I went home now?

2 Excuse me. Could I order a hot drink, please?

3 Is it all right if I use your computer?

4 Is it OK to borrow your dictionary?

5 Am I allowed to ask you a question?

6 May I sit here, please?

a No, not at all. We've finished anyway.

b Oh, I'm afraid it's not my book.

c Oh, I'm so sorry. That seat's taken.

d Yes, please do, but the Internet connection's not working very well.

e Sure. I just hope I'll know the answer!

f Yes, of course, sir. What would you like?

17

Comparatives

Making comparisons of people and things

than, so ... as, as ... as, much, not much

In this unit you learn about how to compare two or more people or things.

Comparative adjectives

You use comparative adjectives to compare one person or thing with another, or with the same person or thing at another time. After a comparative adjective, you often use **than**.

> I am **happier** than I have ever been.
> I've found a **better** hotel with **more comfortable** beds.
> There are **more** people going to university than ever before.

You use **much** and **many** to make a greater comparison.

> It was **much hotter** in Malaga than in Madrid.
> Those jeans are **much more expensive** than the ones I bought.
> There are **many more** people living in London than Manchester.

You use **not much** to say that there is a difference but that the difference is small.

> My brother is **not much taller** than me and he isn't **much more intelligent** either!

Using *as ... as*

You use **as ... as ...** to compare people or things that are similar in some way.

> You're **as bad as** your sister.
> The airport was **as crowded as** ever.
> I am **as good as** she is.

You can make a negative comparison using **not as ... as ...** or **not so ... as ...**.

> The food was**n't as good as** yesterday.
> They are **not as clever as** they appear to be.
> He is **not so old as** I thought.

Exercise 1

Decide if the pairs of sentences have the same meaning.

1 **A** They are much richer than us.
   B We are much poorer than them. ❑

2 **A** My apartment is as big as my cousin's apartment.
   B My cousin's apartment is bigger than my apartment. ❑

3 **A** My new laptop works much faster than my old one.
   B My old laptop was much slower than my new one. ❑

4 **A** Can you explain why we're using a much older version of the software?
   B Can you explain why we're not using the latest version of the software? ❑

5 **A** My working day is much longer than it used to be. ❑
   B I used to work much longer hours than I do now.

6 **A** I speak English much more fluently than I did a year ago. ❑
   B Last year I spoke English just as fluently as I do now.

Exercise 2

Put the correct word in each gap.

| more | further | than | as | much | cooler |

Hi Ellen

I went to the new sports centre at the weekend. It's great! There's a swimming pool which is
¹_____ longer than the swimming pool at college, but I don't think it's quite so
warm ²_____ the college one. It might be one or two degrees ³_____.
It's ⁴_____ expensive to go there and you have to travel ⁵_____, but it's
worth it. You can have different lessons too. We could have tennis lessons together but you're
much better at it ⁶_____ me. What do you think?

Love

Angela

Exercise 3

Which sentences are correct?

1 Sandra's job is much interesting than mine. ❑
2 Why does this report have to be much longer than the last one? ❑
3 This problem is not so difficult than you imagine. ❑
4 I'm much better at maths that my brother is. ❑
5 My grandmother can't walk so fast as she used to. ❑
6 Simon can read French much more quickly than I can. ❑

Exercise 4

Put each sentence into the correct order.

1 possible / as / fast / as / ran / Paula / .

_____

2 his / brother / as / tall / not / John / as / is / .

_____

3 went / this / festival / more / year's / many / people / to / .

_____

4 much / will / the / last / worse / be / weather / than / year / .

_____

5 than / expected / to / better / film / be / it / I / was / the / .

_____

6 park / litter / there / why / before / the / more / is / than / in / ?

_____

Exercise 5

Find the wrong or extra word in each sentence.

1 Mark travels much more further to work than I do.

2 Today's lesson wasn't so interesting than yesterday's.

3 The new teacher explains things much more than clearly.

4 This pizza is more tastier than the one I had last week.

5 More people are taking a winter holiday now than was ten years ago.

6 How much more longer will we have to wait?

Exercise 6

Write the correct form of the word in brackets to complete each sentence.

1 I'm much _____ (tidy) than my sister.

2 The weather is much _____ (bad) than yesterday.

3 He ran more _____ (quick) in the last race.

4 This child is much _____ (intelligent) than we thought.

5 This machine isn't working so _____ (good) these days.

6 I felt much _____ (good) when I got up this morning.

18

Adjective order

Using adjectives in the correct order to describe people and things

In this unit you learn how to describe someone or something using more than one adjective.

Adjective order

Most adjectives can be used in a noun phrase, after determiners and numbers if there are any, or in front of the noun.

> *He had a **beautiful** smile.*
> *She bought a loaf of **white** bread.*
> *Six **new** episodes of the TV show will be filmed.*

You often want to add more information to a noun than you can with one adjective.

When you use more than one adjective, one with a more general meaning such as **good**, **bad**, **nice** or **lovely** usually comes before one with a more specific meaning such as **comfortable**, **clean** or **dirty**.

> *You live in a **nice big** house.*
> *He is a **naughty little** boy.*
> *She was wearing a **beautiful pink** suit.*
> *I sat in a **lovely comfortable** armchair in the corner.*

These adjectives belong to six main types, but you are unlikely ever to use all six types in the same sentence. If you did, you would normally put them in the following order:

size → age → shape → colour → nationality → material

This means that if you want to use an age adjective and a nationality adjective, you put the age adjective first.

> *We met some **young Chinese** girls.*

Similarly, a shape adjective normally comes before a colour adjective.

> *He had **round black** eyes.*

Other combinations of adjectives follow the same order. Note that **material** means any substance, not only cloth.

> *There was a **large round wooden** table in the room.*
> *The man was carrying a **small black plastic** bag.*

Linking adjectives together

When you use two adjectives of the same type, you use **and** to link them. With three or more adjectives, you link the last two with **and**, and put commas after the others.

*The day was **hot and dusty**.*
*The house was **old, damp and smelly**.*
*We felt **hot, tired and thirsty**.*

When you are linking two negative adjectives, you use **or**.

*My job **isn't interesting or well-paid**.*
*We went to see a romantic comedy at the cinema. Unfortunately, it **wasn't funny or romantic**!*

Exercise 1

Put the correct word in each gap.

| comfortable | easy | sandy | and | patient | or | but |

The Belle-vue Hotel

This hotel is both warm [1]_____ welcoming to couples and families. The large,

[2]_____ bedrooms all have a bathroom and views of the sea. The staff are friendly,

kind and [3]_____, and very helpful to new guests.

The Belle-vue Hotel is only a short, [4]_____ walk from the city centre and the long

[5]_____ beach, where you can enjoy all the exciting seaside activities or just sit in

the sun.

Prices at the Belle-vue Hotel aren't high [6]_____ unreasonable, so if you are looking

for a short break in the south of England you should check out their website.

Exercise 2

Put each sentence into the correct order.

1 jacket / Mary / new / yesterday. / bought / yellow / a

_____

2 black / those / clouds / big / look / at / !

_____

3 beautiful / in that / round / shop. / wooden / we saw / table / a

_____

4 look / and / sad / why / Ann / upset / did / yesterday / ?

_____

5 leather / have / gloves / you / black / seen / my / ?

_____

6 with the / Sarah is / woman / beautiful / hair / the / black / long / .

_____

Exercise 3

Which sentences are correct?

1 These black and white photographs are lovely to look at. ❑

2 Is this blue large cardigan yours? ❑

3 I hate driving that car; it's old and dangerous. ❑

4 I really don't like James; he isn't kind or generous. ❑

5 What an old lovely house you have. ❑

6 Do you know that Russian interesting song? ❑

Exercise 4

Find the wrong or extra word in each sentence.

1 Tony is really easy-going and also relaxed.

2 Which flavour yoghurt would you like, blueberry or and strawberry?

3 Who is that tall woman, the one with the large and blue eyes?

4 The food in that restaurant isn't good or not cheap.

5 The most important thing is for you to feel calm, relaxed and too happy.

6 I didn't like that film because it was long and more boring.

Exercise 5

Choose the correct word.

1 Henri Gérard is the young **French / lovely / nice** actor in the latest James Bond movie.

2 The last time I saw Matthew, he was happy **and / if / also** successful.

3 Tomorrow will be a lovely day, warm **though / and / because** sunny.

4 Peter isn't the most interesting **if / also / or** the most exciting person I know.

5 Sharon is the pretty girl with the long, curly, **beautiful / Spanish / brown** hair, near the window.

Exercise 6

Match the two parts.

1 This book looks interesting.	**a** blue eyes, hasn't she?
2 Jackie has just bought a nice	**b** Cold and tired.
3 The actor is tall	**c** and handsome.
4 This soup isn't hot	**d** or tasty.
5 How do you feel after your long walk?	**e** new house.
6 Sally has such big	**f** It is.

19

-ing/-ed adjectives

Adjectives made from parts of verbs

exciting/excited, amazing/amazed, embarrassing/embarrassed, etc.

In this unit you learn how many adjectives are formed from verbs.

If an event, for example a film, is:	a person watching the film will feel:
amazing	amazed
boring	bored
exciting	excited
surprising	surprised
terrifying	terrified
tiring	tired
worrying	worried
frightening	frightened
interesting	interested
shocking	shocked
embarrassing	embarrassed
disappointing	disappointed
confusing	confused
annoying	annoyed
pleasing	pleased

-ing and -ed adjectives

You use many **-ing** adjectives to describe the effect that something has on your feelings, or on the feelings of people in general. For example, if you talk about **a surprising number**, you mean that the number surprises you.

Many **-ed** adjectives describe people's feelings. They have a passive meaning. For example, **a frightened person** is a person who has been frightened by something.

Like other adjectives, **-ing** and **-ed** adjectives can be:

● used in front of a noun

*The children show **shocking** rudeness to their parents.*
*This is the most **terrifying** story ever written.*
*I was thanked by the **satisfied** customer.*
*The **worried** police cancelled the football match.*

- used after linking verbs

  It's **amazing** what they can do.
  The present situation is **terrifying**.
  He felt **satisfied** with all the work he had done.
  My husband was **worried**.

- modified by adverbials such as **quite**, **really** and **very**

  The film was quite **boring**.
  There is nothing very **surprising** in this.
  She was quite **embarrassed** at his behaviour.
  He was a very **disappointed** young man.

A small number of **-ed** adjectives are mainly used after linking verbs such as **be**, **become** or **feel**.

  The Brazilians are **pleased** with the results.
  She was **scared** that they would find her.

Adjective and infinitive

You can use a clause beginning with a **to**-*infinitive* after many adjectives to give more information about something.

  I was **afraid** to go home.
  I was **happy** to see them again.
  The path was **easy** to follow.

Exercise 1

Match the sentence halves.

1 Jenna went for a nice long run and
2 Jack's map had no street names, so
3 Maria didn't get the job she'd wanted, so
4 Archie's sister used his mobile without asking, so
5 Belinda saw her best friend on TV –
6 The boss couldn't answer even a simple question –

a it was confusing.
b it was embarrassing.
c she was tired afterwards.
d it was an amazing programme!
e he was annoyed with her.
f she was disappointed.

Exercise 2

Choose the correct word.

1 Sam was busy reading an **interesting / interested** book.
2 I saw an **amazed / amazing** film on TV last night.
3 Lots of **annoyed / annoying** passengers complained about the train delays.
4 The **exciting / excited** children were talking and laughing happily.
5 We all thought *Car Chase* was a very **disappointing / disappointed** film.
6 A **frightened / frightening** rabbit was sitting quietly in my garden.

Exercise 3

For each question, tick the correct answer.

1 Jack was pleased
   ❏ to see me.
   ❏ for see me.

2 Jon was disappointed to hear
   ❏ he'd passed.
   ❏ he'd failed.

3 Penny wasn't afraid
   ❏ to ask for help.
   ❏ asking for help.

4 It was very difficult
   ❏ to do the work.
   ❏ doing the work.

5 Peter was shocked
   ❏ of hearing the news.
   ❏ to hear the news.

6 Max was
   ❏ surprised to see what happened.
   ❏ surprising to see what happened.

Exercise 4

Put each sentence into the correct order.

1 an / watched / Harry / amazing / match / TV / on / .

   _____

2 afraid / Karen / to / for / ask / help / was / .

   _____

3 is / very / boring / film / this / a / .

   _____

4 visit / interesting / museum / is / to / it / the / .

   _____

5 it / was / exciting / an / game / ?

   _____

6 shocked / hear / to / news / the / Tim / was / .

   _____

Exercise 5

For each question, tick the correct answer.

1 John thought the basketball game was
   ❏ exciting.
   ❏ excited.

2 Sally saw the news on TV and she was
   ❏ shocked.
   ❏ shocking.

3 Karen says the horror film is very
   ❏ frightening.
   ❏ frightened.

4 Sam was happy
   ❏ for giving me some help.
   ❏ to give me some help.

5 Phil finds working an eight-hour day very
   ❏ tired.
   ❏ tiring.

6 My dog is always pleased
   ❏ at seeing me.
   ❏ to see me.

20

Using *-ing* forms as nouns

In this unit you learn about using *-ing* forms as nouns.

Using *-ing* forms as nouns

When you want to talk about an action, activity or process in a general way, you can use a noun that has the same form as the *-ing* participle of a verb.

They can be the subject or object of a clause.

> *Swimming is a great sport.*
> *The closing of so many factories left thousands of people unemployed.*
> *Some people have never done any public speaking.*
> *As a child, his interests were drawing and stamp collecting.*
> *Not being on time is his worst fault.*

You often use an *-ing* noun because it is the only noun form available for certain verbs, such as **eat**, **hear**, **go** and **come**.

> *Eating is an important part of a cruise holiday.*

A few nouns ending in *-ing*, particularly ones referring to leisure activities, are not related to verbs, but are formed from other nouns, or are much commoner than the related verbs. For example, you are more likely to say *We went camping round France* than *We camped round France*. Here is a list of the commonest of these nouns:

boating	skateboarding
mountaineering	snorkelling
canoeing	snowboarding
caravanning	surfing
shopping	windsurfing
sightseeing	yachting

Verbs followed by *-ing* forms

The following verbs can be followed by an *-ing* clause:

describe	enjoy
imagine	miss
dislike	practice
hate	finish
keep	stop
mind	suggest

> *They enjoy working together.*
> *You must keep trying.*
> *I hate not finishing my work on time.*

Exercise 1

Write the missing word in sentence B so that it means the same as sentence A.

1 A I love to play tennis in the summer.

  B _____ tennis in the summer is what I love to do.

2 A I was really disappointed you didn't come to my party.

  B Your not _____ to my party really disappointed me.

3 A Don't talk to me any more. I don't want to listen to you.

  B Stop _____ to me. I don't want to listen to you.

4 A It's not a good idea to drive at night.

  B _____ at night isn't a good idea.

Exercise 2

Complete the sentences by writing one word in each gap.

reading | smoking | flying | opening | doing | making | taking

1 _____ is not good for you, and cigarettes are so expensive.

2 What I enjoy most is _____ books about animals.

3 I love travelling but I hate _____ in a plane.

4 Would you mind me _____ the window? It's very hot in here.

5 _____ a holiday is a good idea. You look so tired.

6 I really don't enjoy studying, and _____ homework is the worst thing.

Exercise 3

Are the highlighted words correct or incorrect in the sentences?

1 To dance ❑ is a good form of exercise.

2 Moving ❑ to a new town is very difficult.

3 Maria suggested **to go** ❑ to the cinema but I was too tired.

4 You don't have to come to the gym, but never **exercising** ❑ is bad for you.

5 Bob looked angry. I think it was because of my **talk** ❑ too much.

6 It's nice **spend** ❑ time with you.

7 Annie, I want you **to help** ❑ me with the dishes after dinner.

Exercise 4

Find the wrong or extra word in each sentence.

1 It's late. Let's finish it cleaning the house tomorrow.

2 How often have I told you to stop to playing that guitar at night?

3 To spending all your money on holiday like this is not a good idea.

4 Please continue to playing the piano. I love listening to the music.

5 Don't talk to me about Joan. Just seeing to her makes me angry.

6 There are lots of things I enjoy doing, but cooking it the dinner isn't one of them.

Exercise 5

Decide if the pairs of sentences have the same meaning.

1 **A** It has started raining.
   B It has started to rain. ❑

2 **A** Reading this book really made me sleepy.
   B I was sleepy so I read this book. ❑

3 **A** Not knowing what time Tim was arriving, I just had to wait.
   B Tim didn't know what time he was arriving, so I just had to wait. ❑

4 **A** Karen is ready to listen to you now.
   B Karen is good at listening to you. ❑

5 **A** Staying in bed too long gives me a headache.
   B I get a headache if I stay in bed too long. ❑

Exercise 6

Which sentences are correct?

1 To lend money to Jack is a silly idea. He will never pay you back. ❑

2 Not having much money, I decided to stay at home and watch TV. ❑

3 We need to talk. Arguing with each other isn't helpful. ❑

4 Sing is what I do when I am bored. ❑

5 Sorry, but there is no smoking allowed in this waiting room. ❑

6 Thank you for your waiting. You can see the doctor now. ❑

Exercise 7

Put each sentence into the correct order.

1 good / for / all / your eyes / that / isn't / reading / .

_____

2 hobbies / are / my / the / singing and / favourite / piano / playing / .

_____

3 cooking / TV / hungry / programmes / watching / me / on / makes / .

_____

4 becoming / the best / a / thing / I ever / teacher / did. / was

_____

5 I agreed / going / a party / Peter / and / to / suggested / .

_____

6 loves / hates / listening to / music but / playing it / Thomas / he / .

_____

21

Nouns and indefinite pronouns + *to-infinitive*

Using nouns and verbs to make subjects

In this unit you learn how to use nouns and words like **somewhere** and **no one**.

Somewhere, anywhere, nowhere

You use **somewhere** to talk about a place without saying exactly where you mean.

> *They live **somewhere** near Brighton.*
> *I'm not going home yet. I have to go **somewhere** else first.*

You don't usually use **somewhere** in negative sentences. Don't say, for example, ~~I couldn't see him somewhere~~. Say:

> *I couldn't see him **anywhere**.*

You can also say:

> *I could see him **nowhere**.*

Something, anything, nothing

You use **something** to refer to an object or situation without saying exactly what it is.

> *I saw **something** in the shadows.*
> *There's **something** strange about her.*

You don't usually use **something** as part of the object of a negative sentence. Don't say, for example, ~~We haven't had something to eat~~. You say:

> *We haven't had **anything** to eat.*

You can also say:

> *We have had **nothing** to eat.*

Some verbs are followed by an object and a **to**-*infinitive* clause. The object of the verb is the subject of the **to**-*infinitive* clause.

Verbs of saying and thinking

> *I asked her **to explain**.*
> *They advised us **not to wait** around too much longer.*

Other verbs

> *I could get someone else **to do it**.*
> *I didn't want him **to go**.*

Using nouns and infinitives

A **to**-*infinitive* clause is often placed after nouns in order to show what the thing referred to is intended to do.

> *The government of Mexico set up a programme **to develop** new ways of farming.*
> *They need people **to work** in the factories.*

You can refer to something or someone that should or can have something done to them by using a clause containing a **to**-*infinitive* after a noun or indefinite pronoun.

> *I make notes in the back of my diary of things **to be repaired or replaced**.*
> *I'll go out when I've had something **to eat**.*

Exercise 1

Match the sentence halves.

1	It's a situation	**a**	to avoid.
2	The person to ask	**b**	to ask for advice?
3	There's nothing	**c**	to add?
4	I can do nothing	**d**	to help right now.
5	Is there anyone	**e**	to do around here.
6	Is there something you'd like	**f**	is your teacher.

Exercise 2

Which sentences are correct?

1 They don't want nothing to drink. ❑
2 Have you got anything to read? ❑
3 I've found anywhere nice to eat – an Italian restaurant. ❑
4 Can you see anywhere to sit? ❑
5 I've got something important to tell you. ❑
6 We need anyone to tell us what we should do. ❑

Exercise 3

Choose the correct word or phrase.

1 I can't find anything interesting **to / I** read in this magazine.
2 This is a great band to **dancing / dance** to.
3 This is the most important question **to ask / for asking**.
4 It was definitely a holiday **that will remember / to remember**.
5 There's nothing **can / to** do around here; it's boring!
6 You can have **that / anything** you like to eat.
7 I need something **to / which** put all these old clothes in.

Exercise 4

Find the wrong or extra word in each sentence.

1 You need a friend for to talk to when you have a problem.

2 The desert in the south west is an interesting area to visit it.

3 I've got nothing which to add to my previous statement.

4 Can you give anything to us help the homeless?

5 In my opinion, it's a good business worth to invest in.

6 Is there anything where to put rubbish in?

Exercise 5

Write one word in sentence B so that it means the same as sentence A.

1 A I'm looking for a place where I can hide the children's presents.
  B I'm looking for _____ to hide the children's presents.

2 A There isn't a spare seat.
  B There's nowhere to _____.

3 A Is there a person who can give me some advice?
  B Is there anyone to _____ me?

4 A How can I help?
  B What can I do _____ help?

5 A Don't worry about anything.
  B There's _____ to worry about.

6 A I'm going to tell you some very important news.
  B I've got _____ very important to say.

Exercise 6

Decide if the pairs of sentences have the same meaning.

1 A There was nobody to ask.
  B I couldn't find anyone to ask. ☐

2 A You've no one to blame but yourself.
  B It's your own fault. ☐

3 A There wasn't anyone interesting to talk to at the party.
  B I had an interesting talk with someone at the party. ☐

4 A There was nothing extra to pay.
  B We had to pay extra. ☐

5 A Is there anywhere to get a cup of coffee?
  B Where can I get a cup of coffee? ☐

6 A The students need something to eat after a football match.
  B The students are hungry when they've been playing football. ☐

wh-clauses

Using phrases with *wh*-pronouns to make objects

where, who, why, which, how, what

In this unit you learn about a different way to ask questions.

A bike has been stolen! Imagine you are a policeman or policewoman. Use the table below to make some statements and ask some questions.

Statement	Wh-pronoun	Wh-clause
I wonder	where	the thief has taken the bike.
I don't know	who	took the bike.
I don't understand	why	the bike was stolen
Tell me	which one	of these men took the bike.
Question		
Shall we discuss	how	we are going to find the bike?
Do you know	what	the thief looks like?
Did he tell you	where	he was going?
Have you decided	where	to look for him?

Wh-questions

These are questions in which someone asks for information about an event or situation. **Wh-questions** cannot be answered with *yes* or *no*. When you report a **wh-question**, you use a **wh-word** at the beginning of the reported clause.

*He asked **where** I was going.*
*I asked **how** they had got there so quickly.*

Other verbs can be used before clauses beginning with **wh-words**, because they refer to knowing, learning or mentioning one of the circumstances of an event or situation.

*She doesn't know **what** we were talking about.*
*I don't understand **how** we can manage without her.*
*I wonder **what's** happened.*

Here is a list of other verbs that can be used before clauses beginning with **wh-words**:

explain	guess	decide	say
know	realize	describe	think
forget	imagine	discover	understand
learn	remember	discuss	wonder

Wonder

The verb **wonder** is usually used to say that someone is thinking about something and is trying to guess or understand more about it. **Wonder** is often used with *wh*-clauses.

I wonder what she looks like.
I wonder which hotel it was.

Exercise 1

Complete the sentences by writing one word in each gap.

where | why | who | what | which | how

1 What about her reason for leaving? Does anyone have any idea _____ she decided to go?

2 I don't even know _____ we're meeting. It could be anywhere in town.

3 Do you know _____ she spoke to?

4 There are two books on the subject. Did she tell you _____ one to get?

5 I don't know _____ they're getting here, whether they're coming on the bus or the train.

6 I've no idea _____ to cook for dinner.

Exercise 2

Match the two parts.

1 Do you know why she left?

2 Did you arrange where to meet?

3 You can have any of these scarves. Just tell me which you prefer.

4 Did Karl say who he was meeting?

5 Have you decided what to do today?

6 Do you know how they're getting here?

a The blue one.

b Yes, we're going swimming.

c Yes, she was unhappy here.

d Yes, the Rainbow Café.

e By bike, I expect.

f Helena and Polly.

Exercise 3

Put each sentence into the correct order.

1 know / do / I / to / what / don't / .

_____

2 that man / where / I've / works / discovered / .

_____

3 what / wonder / happen / will / I / .

_____

4 explained / she was / Susie / why / laughing / .

_____

5 know / I don't / which / to / dress / buy / .

_____

6 remember / said / do / you / who / that / ?

_____

Exercise 4

Choose the correct word.

Terry received an email from his favourite film star, inviting him to have dinner with her. She wanted him to tell her [1]**where / what / which** he would do with a million pounds. Terry was amazed, and immediately agreed. He received another email, telling him [2]**where / who / how** they would meet – at the most expensive restaurant in the city – and when: the following evening.

Terry couldn't think [3]**who / how / why** the film star wanted to give him so much money. He also wondered [4]**how / where / what** to dress, and he bought an expensive new suit, so that he looked smart.

The next evening he went to the restaurant, and told a waiter [5]**who / which / what** he was meeting. The waiter laughed. There was no film star in the restaurant – one of Terry's friends had played a trick on him. He never found out [6]**who / where / which** friend it was!

Exercise 5

Which sentences are correct?

1 I don't know why is she crying. ❑
2 I didn't understand what he was saying. ❑
3 Just tell me which one you prefer. ❑
4 I tried to explain how did the accident happen. ❑
5 Do you know who Laura was meeting tonight? ❑
6 Ian didn't say where was he going. ❑

Exercise 6

Complete the sentences by writing one word in each gap.

1 We've no idea _____ will happen now.
2 No one can understand _____ he did that. Perhaps he was trying to impress his girlfriend.
3 I asked Greg _____ of the two laptops was better.
4 Anna and I have finally decided _____ to have the party.
5 She explained _____ the machine worked – something to do with pipes and water.
6 I remembered the words but I couldn't remember _____ had said them.

23

Relative pronouns

Using *wh*-pronouns when giving more information about people and things

who, which, that, whose, when, where

In this unit you learn about using *wh*-**pronouns** to give further information about people and things.

Defining relative clauses

You use defining relative clauses to give information that helps to identify the person or thing you are talking about.

> *The man **who** you met yesterday was my brother.*
> *The car **that** crashed belonged to Paul.*

When you are talking about people, you use **that** or **who** in the relative clause.

> *He was the man **that** bought my house.*
> *You are the only person here **who** knows me.*

When you are talking about things, you use **that** or **which** in the relative clause.

> *There was ice cream **that** Mum had made herself.*
> *I'll tell you the first thing **which** I can remember.*

You use **whose** in relative clauses to indicate who something belongs to or relates to. You normally use **whose** for people, not for things.

> *A child **whose** mother had left him was crying loudly.*
> *We have only told the people **whose** work is good enough.*

You can use **when** and **where** in defining relative clauses after certain nouns. You use **when** after **time** or time words such as **day** or **year**. You use **where** after **place** or place words such as **room** or **street**.

> *This is the year **when** profits should increase.*
> *He showed me the place **where** they work.*
> *That was the room **where** I did my homework.*

Non-defining relative clauses

You use non-defining relative clauses to give extra information about the person or thing you are talking about. The information is not needed to identify that person or thing. In the example below, **who was always early** gives extra information about Professor Marvin. This is a non-defining relative clause, because it is not needed to identify the person you are talking about. You already know that you are talking about Professor Marvin.

*Professor Marvin, **who** was always early, was there already.*

Note that in written English, a non-defining relative clause is usually separated from the main clause by a comma, or by two commas.

*British Rail, **which has started an enquiry**, said one train was badly damaged.*

When you are talking about people, you use **who** in the relative clause.

*I went to the cinema with Mary, **who you met**.*

When you are talking about things, you use **which** as the subject or object of a non-defining relative clause.

*I am teaching at the local college, **which is just over the road**.*
*He had a lot of money, **which he spent mainly on cars**.*

You do not normally use **that** in non-defining relative clauses.

You can also use a non-defining relative clause beginning with **which** to say something about the whole situation described in a main clause.

*I never met Brendan again, **which was a pity**.*
*She was a little nervous, **which was understandable**.*
*Small computers need only small amounts of power, **which means that they will run on small batteries**.*

You can use **when** and **where** in non-defining relative clauses after expressions of time or place.

*This happened in 1957, **when I was still a baby**.*
*She has just come back from a holiday in Crete, **where Alex and I went last year**.*

Using a participle instead of a *wh*-word

You use an *-ing* clause after a noun to say what someone or something is doing or was doing at a particular time.

*The young girl **sitting** opposite him was his daughter.*
*Most of the people **walking** in the park were teenagers.*

You can also use an *-ing* clause after a noun to say what a person or thing does generally, rather than at a particular time.

*The men **working** there were not very friendly.*

Exercise 1

Complete the sentences by writing 'who' or 'whose' in each gap.

1 These are all the Spanish authors _____ books I've read.

2 My cousin _____ lives in Rome is coming over next week.

3 Do you know anyone _____ wants to buy a bike?

4 Do you remember that guy _____ father was an actor?

5 The people _____ work there all seem very nice.

6 It's important to find a partner _____ values you respect.

Exercise 2

Write the missing words in sentence B so that it means the same as sentence A. Be careful with commas!

1 **A** I first visited New York when I was a child, and I'm going to move there next month.
  B Next month I'm going to move to New _____ I first visited when I was a child.

2 **A** My wife's job is very well-paid and she thinks we should buy a more expensive house.
  B My _____ thinks we should buy a more expensive house.

3 **A** One of my cousins lives by the sea and he has invited me to spend the summer with him.
  B My _____ has invited me to spend the summer with him.

4 **A** Stephen was born in the city of Bristol, and when he was quite old he went back to live there.
  B When Stephen was quite old he went back to live in _____ – Bristol.

Exercise 3

Match the two sentence halves.

1 Sam passed all his exams, which	**a** is great news.
2 It's a dish that	**b** is really dangerous.
3 This film is by the director whose	**c** my mother used to make when I was little.
4 He cycles without a helmet, which	**d** my father used to play on his guitar.
5 It's a song that	**e** work I most admire.
6 The music was played by a band whose	**f** members were all under fifteen.

Exercise 4

Are the highlighted words correct or incorrect in the sentences?

1 That's the club **which** ❑ I met Johnny.

2 That's the guy **that** ❑ I told you about.

3 2009 was the year **where** ❑ we visited Japan.

4 That's the guy **who** ❑ I told you about.

5 That's the school **where** ❑ my father teaches.

6 Ian is the guy **who** ❑ girlfriend is Polish.

Exercise 5

Which sentences are correct?

1 Did you find the phone number that you needed? ❑

2 Did you finish the document you were working on? ❑

3 That's the waitress served me last time I ate here. ❑

4 They're going to the village which we stayed last year. ❑

5 Peter is the guy that he was going out with Eva. ❑

6 Was Michelle the woman who was wearing a red dress? ❑

Exercise 6

Put the correct word in each gap.

whose	who	when	who	where	which

Hi Patrick!

Are you feeling better this morning? I hope so. We missed you at Ian's party last night. That guy
has so many friends! The room ¹_____ they had the party was huge and it was still
full. Do you remember Ellie, that tall girl ²_____ works in Greens,

³_____ dad used to teach you at college? She was there! She asked where you were,

⁴_____ I thought you would like to know. And guess what? Ian knows a celebrity!

That guy ⁵_____ plays guitar for the Red Ants was there. Isn't that cool? Ian met him

last summer ⁶_____ he was travelling in Turkey.

Love

Sophie

Exercise 7

For each question, tick the correct answer(s).

1 That's the singer
   ❑ whose girlfriend I met at Sally's party.
   ❑ which girlfriend I met at Sally's party.
   ❑ that girlfriend I met at Sally's party.

2 That's a song
   ❑ who reminds me of my time in Spain.
   ❑ which reminds me of my time in Spain.
   ❑ that reminds me of my time in Spain.

3 He's the only person
   ❑ which can help me.
   ❑ who can help me.
   ❑ that can help me.

4 He shouted at me,
   ❑ that really upset me.
   ❑ which really upset me.
   ❑ who really upset me.

24

Have/get something done
Talking about actions you arrange for other people to take

In this unit you learn how to talk about things you arrange for other people to do. The forms you learn are also used to talk about some negative things that people can do to you when you don't want them to.

Janice	We've just **had** our house **painted**.
Phil	Oh, I painted my house myself. I can't afford to **get** someone else **to do** it.

Actions done to you

You can use an object and an **-ed** participle after **have** or **get** when you want to say that someone arranges for something to be done. **Have** is slightly more formal.

> *I've just **had** my hair **cut**. Do you like it?*
> *We must **get** the car **repaired**.*

You also use **have** and **get** with an object and an **-ed** participle to say that something happens to someone, especially if it is unpleasant.

> *She **had** her bag **stolen**. (= A thief stole her bag)*
> *He **got** his car **broken into** at the weekend. (= A thief broke into his car)*

Uses of *got*

Get is a very common verb that has several different meanings.

- In informal English, **get** is sometimes used instead of **be** to form the passive.
  > *Our car **gets cleaned** every weekend.*
  > *He **got killed** in a plane crash.*

- **Get** is often used to mean **become**.
  > *The sun shone and I **got** very hot.*
  > *I was **getting** quite hungry.*

- **Get** is used for describing movement. You use **get** instead of **go** when you are describing a movement that involves difficulty.

    *They had to **get** across the field without being seen.*
    *I don't think we can **get** over that wall.*

- **Get** is also used in front of **in**, **into**, **on** and **out** to talk about entering and leaving vehicles and buildings.

    *I **got** into my car and drove into town.*
    *I **got** out of there as fast as possible*

Exercise 1

Choose the correct word.

1 Debbie has had her bedroom **painting / painted** bright blue.

2 We need to **have / had** the car looked at – it's making a strange noise.

3 Lucy **had / has** her hair cut every three weeks because she likes it really short at the moment.

4 Sam will have his photo **taken / took** by a top photographer if he wins the modelling competition.

5 Dave had his bike **stole / stolen** the day after he bought it!

6 Dylan and Sheena are planning to have some work **did / done** on their house to make it larger.

Exercise 2

Match the sentence halves.

1 My suit is dirty so I must

2 My watch has broken so I'll have to

3 My moustache doesn't suit me so I want to

4 My story won a writing competition and I'm going to

5 My kitchen is old-fashioned so I might

a have it redesigned.

b have it cleaned.

c have it shaved off.

d have it published.

e have it repaired.

Exercise 3

Which sentences are correct?

1 I finally got my homework finish at midnight. ❑

2 Although his hair is really long, he doesn't want to get it cut. ❑

3 Get your feet off the sofa! ❑

4 If you don't lock your bike, you might get stolen. ❑

5 She couldn't get the door to open. ❑

6 When I was in the park, I got Amy and her new dog seen. ❑

Exercise 4

Are the highlighted words correct or incorrect in this text?

When we moved into the house where I live now, we had to **have** ❑ a lot of work carried out on it. First, we didn't like the old kitchen and bathroom, so we had **it** ❑ both replaced. Then we had some repairs **did** ❑ to the roof and we **got** ❑ the whole house redecorated. We're still making changes now. At the moment, **we're having** ❑ our garden cleared and planted. I'd like to have a swimming pool **build** ❑ out there too, but Mum and Dad just laugh when I suggest that to them!

Exercise 5

Write the missing words in sentence B so that it means the same as sentence A.

1 A I went to the art store so someone there could print my photos for me.
   B I _____ my photos printed at the art store.

2 A Katrina wants someone to make her wedding dress by hand.
   B Katrina wants to have her wedding dress _____ by hand.

3 A Someone is checking the brakes on Greg's car.
   B Greg _____ the brakes on his car checked.

4 A Would you like someone to wrap this gift for you, sir?
   B Would you like to have this gift _____, sir?

Exercise 6

Find the wrong or extra word in each sentence.

1 Where do you get it your hair done?
2 Can I have got the books delivered to a different address, please?
3 My eyes are hurting – I need to get them have tested.
4 Jack had a tooth was taken out at the dentist's this morning.
5 You must get to those shoes mended!
6 Get you that sheep out of my garden!

25

Verbs that are used together

Hear, see, want, need

hear/see/want/need + -ing

hear/see + object + verb

In this unit you learn some more verb forms with *-ing* and **to**.

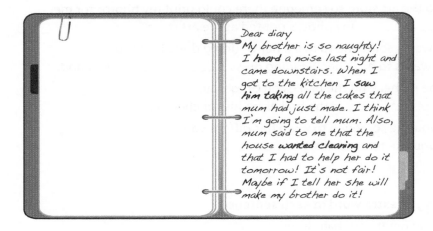

Dear diary
My brother is so naughty!
I **heard** a noise last night and
came downstairs. When I
got to the kitchen I **saw**
him taking all the cakes that
mum had just made. I think
I'm going to tell mum. Also,
mum said to me that the
house **wanted cleaning** and
that I had to help her do it
tomorrow! It's not fair!
Maybe if I tell her she will
make my brother do it!

Hear and *see*

You can use an *-ing* form with **hear** and **see** to show that someone was aware of something that was continuing to take place.

> He **heard** Hajime shouting and laughing.
> I could **hear** him crying.

You can use an infinitive without **to** after **heard** or **saw** to show that someone was aware of a complete event or action.

> I **heard** him open the door.
> I **heard** Amy say something.
> She **saw** him fall down the stairs.

Want doing

In British English, in conversation and in less formal writing, **want** has another meaning. If something wants doing, there is a need for it to be done.

> We've got a few jobs that **want doing** in the garden.
> The windows **wanted cleaning**.

Need with *-ing* forms

You can use **need** with an *-ing* form to say that something should have something done to it. For example, rather than *The cooker needs to be cleaned*, you can say:

> *The cooker **needs cleaning**.*
> *The plan **needs improving**.*
> *We made a list of things that **needed doing**.*

Exercise 1

Choose the correct word or phrase.

Can you see your house ¹**to fall / falling** down around you?

Does everything want ²**fixing / to fix** but you don't have the time or expertise to do it yourself? Let us take all your worries away and make your house as good as new.

Whether it's a burst pipe that needs ³**repair / to be repaired**, a wall that needs ⁴**rebuild / to be rebuilt** or a shed that wants ⁵**pulling down / pulled down**, no job is too big or too small.

And you needn't take our word for it. Just visit our website to see what customers are ⁶**to say / saying** about our work.

Exercise 2

Decide if the pairs of sentences have the same meaning.

1 **A** I heard the man cry.
   B I heard the man crying. ☐

2 **A** I heard you had a birthday party the other day.
   B I heard you having a birthday party the other day. ☐

3 **A** Jenny saw the broken window.
   B Jenny saw the window breaking. ☐

4 **A** Mark, your hair wants cutting.
   B Mark, your hair needs to be cut. ☐

5 **A** Joel wanted Kate to do the job.
   B Joel wanted the job doing for Kate. ☐

Exercise 3

Match the two parts.

1 The roof needs   a cutting. It's very long.

2 My hair wants   b to be cleaned. I did it yesterday.

3 I didn't hear   c you running in the park the other day. You must be fit!

4 I heard   d fixing. Shall I call someone to do it?

5 I saw   e you come into the room. You gave me a surprise.

6 My bedroom doesn't need   f people screaming loudly and then I saw two men with a gun. It was frightening.

Exercise 4

For each question, tick the incorrect answer.

1 Hazel didn't see

❑ the branch falling before it hit her.
❑ the branch to fall before it hit her.
❑ the branch fall before it hit her.

2 The walls

❑ want repainting before we sell the house.
❑ need to be painted before we sell the house.
❑ want to be repainted before we sell the house.

3 Steve heard

❑ the dog to bark.
❑ the dog barking.
❑ the dog bark.

4 My mother wanted

❑ me to go to the Olympics, but she couldn't get me tickets.
❑ to go to the Olympics, but she couldn't get tickets.
❑ us going to the Olympics, but we couldn't get tickets.

5 That cut needed

❑ stitching. You should have gone to the hospital.
❑ being stitched. You should have gone to the hospital.
❑ a doctor to stitch it. You should have gone to the hospital.

Exercise 5

Put each sentence into the correct order.

1 to be / football socks / smelly / washed / those / need / .

_____

2 floor / dirty / wants / this / cleaning / .

_____

3 the man / you / did / steal the bag / see / ?

_____

4 Tracy / the phone / answer it / heard / ringing, but she couldn't / .

_____

5 in time to see / the sun / Josh wanted / rising / to get up / .

_____

6 you could almost / breaking / he missed / hear his heart / her so much / .

_____

Exercise 6

Are the highlighted words correct or incorrect in this text?

Buying a piano

It's always wonderful to hear a piano **being** ❑ played skilfully and many children often want **learning** ❑, but where should you buy a piano and what should you bear in mind when you do so? First of all, you need **to be heard** ❑ a lot of different pianos so that you can decide which instrument's tone you like the best.

Secondly, you should have a budget in mind. If you have seen a professional pianist **to perform** ❑, it's likely that they were playing a grand piano. Although these tend to have the best sound, few people have the money or space to invest in them.

Thirdly, think about where you want **to put** ❑ a piano in your home. If you live in a first-floor flat, you might find it difficult to get a large piano up the stairs!

Finally, if you decide to get a second-hand piano, make sure you ask what needs **done** ❑ before you commit to buying it. If a piano hasn't been played for a while it often wants **tuning** ❑, which is expensive. Make sure you ask for the price of the piano to be reduced to take this into account.

Exercise 7

For each sentence, tick the correct ending.

1 Before we move into the house,
  ❑ it needs to clean from top to bottom.
  ❑ it needs cleaning from top to bottom.
  ❑ it needs be cleaned from top to bottom.

2 You need to have a wash before we go out,
  ❑ and your hair wants brushing.
  ❑ and your hair wants to be brushing.
  ❑ and your hair wants to brush.

3 Did you
  ❑ hear him come in last night?
  ❑ hear him to come in last night?
  ❑ hear him to be coming in last night?

4 Can I leave you with a list
  ❑ of jobs that need to do?
  ❑ of jobs that need to be doing?
  ❑ of jobs that need doing?

5 Lara was sitting by the window
  ❑ and she saw the children to play in the garden.
  ❑ and she saw the children playing in the garden.
  ❑ and she saw the children to be playing in the garden.

6 There's nothing wrong with the desk
  ❑ except that one of the drawer handles wants to be fixing.
  ❑ except that one of the drawer handles wants to fix.
  ❑ except that one of the drawer handles wants fixing.

26

Prepositions

Prepositions for talking about the purpose of actions or things

for, with, as well as, rather than, except for, besides, apart from

In this unit you learn how to use some more prepositions. You can use them to say why or how things are done.

For

You use **for** in front of a noun phrase or **-ing** form when you state the purpose of an object, action or activity.

> *Some planes are **for** internal travel, others are **for** international flights.*
> *The bowl had been used **for** mixing flour and water.*

You use **for** in front of a noun phrase when you are saying why someone does something.

> *We stopped **for** lunch by the side of the road.*
> *I went to the store **for** a newspaper.*

With

If you do something **with** a tool or object, you do it using that tool or object.

> *Clean the floor **with** a mop.*
> *He pushed back his hair **with** his hand.*

You use **with** after verbs like **fight** or **argue**. For example, if two people are fighting, you can say that one person is fighting with the other.

> *He was always fighting **with** his brother.*

Prepositions with the meaning *in addition to*

As well as

If you say that something is true of one person or thing **as well as** another, you are emphasizing that it is true not only of the second person or thing but also of the first one.

> *Women, **as well as men**, have the right to work.*
> *She's great at her job. She manages the accounts **as well as** ordering the equipment.*

Along with

You use **along with** when you want to say **as well as**.

> ***Along with** everyone else, I wanted to try the new chocolate bar.*

Prepositions with the meaning *not*

Rather than

Rather than is used to link words or expressions of the same type. You use **rather than** when you have said what is true and you want to compare it with what is not true.

> *It made him frightened **rather than** angry.*
> *You will get a free meal **rather than** any pay.*

Except for

You use **except for** in front of a noun phrase when you are mentioning something that prevents a statement from being completely true.

> *The classroom was silent, **except for** the sound of pens on paper.*
> *The room was very cold and, **except for** Mao, completely empty.*

Besides

Besides means **in addition to** or **as well as**.

> *Which languages do you know **besides** Arabic and English?*
> *There was only one person **besides** Jacques who knew Lorraine.*

Apart from

You use **apart from** when you mention an exception to a statement that you are making.

> ***Apart from** Ann, the car was empty.*
> *She had no money, **apart from** the five pounds that Christopher had given her.*

Exercise 1

Match the sentence halves.

1 I went to the park for	a	a large stone.
2 It's better to go online for	b	a piece of card.
3 We saved £1,000 for	c	information about prices.
4 She mended the book with	d	printing photographs.
5 We use this paper for	e	a holiday.
6 They broke the window with	f	some fresh air.

Exercise 2

Choose the correct word or phrase.

1 You will study psychology **as well as / other than** sociology on this course.
2 It's a great city to live in **except / apart** from the weather.
3 Do you play any sports other **than / besides** football and hockey?
4 **Besides / In addition** to his city flat, he has a holiday house on the coast.
5 Business Studies, **along / apart** with Computer Studies, is the most popular course at this college.
6 Everyone came to the party **except / along** for James.

Exercise 3

Put the correct phrase in each gap.

It's for opening cans. | It's for opening a car door. | It's for painting. | It's for measuring things. | It's for cutting bread. | It's for keeping things cold.

1 _____

2 _____

3 _____

4 _____

5 _____

6 _____

Exercise 4

Are the highlighted words correct or incorrect in the sentences?

1 Everybody loves ice cream except **from** ☐ my sister.

2 Let's take a taxi rather **than** ☐ the bus.

3 You open your hotel door **with** ☐ this card.

4 He phoned me **with** ☐ a chat about work.

5 What do you use that spoon **at** ☐? It's an unusual shape.

6 My brother was in the swimming pool **along** ☐ some of his friends.

Exercise 5

Put the correct word or phrase in each gap.

| as well as | rather than | in addition | with | except for | for |

Online Sports Management Course

This course offers training about health and fitness [1]_____ business.
[2]_____ to weekly lessons, the course includes short films online. You will be taught
about equipment [3]_____ measuring heart rate, etc. You must complete seven
pieces of coursework. Your teacher will make comments on all your work [4]_____
your end-of-course exam. You will get a final grade [5]_____ comments on this exam.
You will receive the comments online. You can open the comments page [6]_____ a
special password that we will send you.

Exercise 6

Decide if the pairs of sentences have the same meaning.

1 **A** Everyone enjoyed the festival except for Tony.
   B Everyone enjoyed the festival apart from Tony. ❏

2 **A** I'd like salad rather than chips with my meal.
   B I'd like salad as well as chips with my meal. ❏

3 **A** Along with everyone else on the flight, I waited an hour for my luggage.
   B No one else on the flight had to wait an hour for their luggage except me. ❏

4 **A** Besides doing sport, she eats a healthy diet.
   B She eats healthily and she does sport. ❏

5 **A** I phone my friends rather than text them.
   B Besides phoning my friends, I text them. ❏

6 **A** I don't like most kinds of meat except for chicken.
   B I don't like chicken but I like other kinds of meat. ❏

Exercise 7

For each sentence, tick the correct ending.

1 You can use this knife
   ❏ with cutting bread.
   ❏ for cutting bread.

2 Paul had a bad day at school
   ❏ and then argued with his brother
     when he got home.
   ❏ and then argued at his brother
     when he got home.

3 Anya works 15 hours a week
   ❏ as well as looking after the children.
   ❏ as well as to look after the children.

4 None of them wanted dessert
   ❏ besides David who ordered a slice of
     chocolate cake.
   ❏ apart from David who ordered a slice of
     chocolate cake.

5 Bella says she would prefer
   ❏ to pick the children up now rather than later.
   ❏ to pick the children up now apart from later.

6 She kicked the chair over
   ❏ along with her foot.
   ❏ with her foot.

27

Some/any/nobody/so/such

In this unit you learn how to use **some**, **any**, **nobody**, **so**, **such** correctly in sentences.

Using -body and -one

You use indefinite pronouns when you want to refer to people or things without saying exactly who or what they are. The pronouns ending in **-body** and **-one** refer to people.

> *I was there for over an hour before **anybody** came.*
> *It had to be **someone** with a car.*

When an indefinite pronoun is the subject, it always takes a singular verb, even when it refers to more than one person or thing.

> ***No one** knows that.*
> *Is **anybody** there?*

Someone and somebody

You use indefinite pronouns beginning with **some-** in:

- affirmative clauses
  > ***Somebody** shouted.*
  > *I want to introduce you to **someone**.*

- questions expecting the answer 'yes'
  > *Can you get **someone** to do it?*

Anyone and anybody

You use indefinite pronouns beginning with **any-**:

- as the subject or object in statements
  > ***Anyone** knows that you need a licence.*

- in both affirmative and negative questions
  > *Does **anybody** agree with me?*
  > *Won't **anyone** help me?*

You do not use them as the subject of a negative statement. You do not say *Anybody can't come in.*

No one and nobody

You use indefinite pronouns beginning with **no-** in negative sentences:

> ***No one** likes him.*

Else

You can use **else** to refer to people, things or places other than those that have been mentioned.

> *Everyone else is downstairs.*
> *No one else believes me.*

So and *such*

You use **so** and **such** to emphasize a quality that someone or something has. **So** can be followed by an adjective, an adverb or a noun phrase beginning with **many**, **much**, **few** or **little**.

> *John is so interesting to talk to.*
> *The world is changing so quickly.*
> *I want to do so many different things.*

Such is followed by a singular noun phrase with **a**, or a plural noun phrase.

> *There was such a noise we couldn't hear.*
> *They said such horrible things.*

Remember!

Note that **no one** is written as two words, or sometimes with a hyphen: **no-one**. Also, if you use **nobody** or **no one** you do not use another negative word in the same clause. You do not say *There wasn't nobody.*

Exercise 1

Complete the sentences by writing *so* or *such* in each gap.

1 The flight to Los Angeles was _____ long that I don't want to fly direct again.

2 With _____ nice food at home, we don't need to go to a restaurant.

3 Katie has _____ a big cupboard that she can put all her old things there.

4 David is _____ clever, he finished his homework before I did.

5 Those shoes are _____ pretty I just have to buy them.

6 I am really embarrassed because that was _____ a big mistake.

Exercise 2

Which sentences are correct?

1 I need anyone to help me hand out these books. Sam, can you help me? ☐

2 Has anybody seen Donald this morning? He's late. ☐

3 Sally was really upset yesterday. She didn't want to talk to nobody. ☐

4 There is anybody on the phone for you, Richard. I didn't get the
  name, but it's about your car. ☐

5 Anyone who saw the accident should call the police ☐

6 I saw somebody I knew at the cinema last night – an old friend. ☐

Exercise 3

Put the correct word or phrase in each gap.

> anyone else | someone | someone else | nobody else | no one | anybody

The tennis club invited a famous tennis player to talk to club members. He talked for a while, then asked if [1]_____ had any questions. For a moment or two, [2]_____ spoke. Then [3]_____ asked how he had started to play tennis. He replied that he had watched a tennis match on television when he was six years old, and asked his parents to buy him a children's racket. They gave him one, and he joined a tennis club for children.

Very soon he could play much better than [4]_____ in the club. His parents were surprised, because [5]_____ in the family played tennis. Before long, he wanted an adult tennis racket, and he gave his small one to [6]_____ who belonged to the club – and that child also became a famous tennis player when she was an adult.

Exercise 4

Match the questions and answers.

1 What would you like to drink?
2 Did you see anyone we know in town?
3 Did you call me just now?
4 There's somebody at the door.
5 There was nobody at the beach yesteday.
6 Dr Cramer is on holiday.

a Shall I answer it?
b Can I see someone else?
c No, it was someone else I wanted.
d That was lucky for you.
e Anything, I don't mind.
f No, no one.

Exercise 5

Choose the correct word.

The party

The reason for the party was to celebrate Joseph's new job. We invited [1]**so / such** many people we weren't sure there was enough room in the house! We asked David to take Joseph to a football match because the party was a surprise. We bought drinks and food and decorated the house. The fridge was [2]**so / such** full that we couldn't close the door properly.

At six o'clock our friends started arriving. I was preparing the food in the kitchen so I asked [3]**someone / anyone** else to open the door every time the bell rang. By 8.30 everybody was there except David and Joseph. [4]**No one / Anyone** knew where they were and we couldn't telephone David because nobody had his phone number. We were all [5]**so / such** worried. [6]**Somebody / Nobody** said we should ring the police and [7]**someone / no one** else said we should go out and look for them. Just then, the door opened and David and Joseph walked in. They'd lost the keys to David's car and had had to walk all the way home!

Exercise 6

Decide if the pairs of sentences have the same meaning.

1 **A** I didn't know Noor lived such a long way away.
   B I didn't know Noor lived so far away. ☐

2 **A** Somebody told me that Tim and Pat were getting married.
   B Nobody told me that Tim and Pat were getting married. ☐

3 **A** Does anyone have any money they can lend me?
   B Can someone lend me some money? ☐

4 **A** I have so many shoes I don't know where to put them all.
   B I know just where I have put all of my shoes. ☐

5 **A** I thought I saw Thomas in town but it was somebody else.
   B I saw Thomas in town but I didn't see anybody else. ☐

Exercise 7

Are the highlighted words correct or incorrect in the sentences?

1 Betty didn't tell **nobody** ☐ about her holiday plans.

2 This is **such** ☐ an easy game that **anybody** ☐ can play it.

3 It was **so** ☐ dark on the road, Phil couldn't see **somebody** ☐.

4 This house is empty and there is **no one** ☐ living in it.

5 Stop playing with that knife, you could hurt **anybody** ☐. It's **such** ☐ sharp.

6 I don't want to clean up that room; **someone** ☐ else can do it.

Exercise 8

Write one missing word in sentence B so that it means the same as sentence A.

1 **A** That accident was really serious but fortunately everyone was OK.
   B That accident was really serious but fortunately no one _____ hurt.

2 **A** My bag was really heavy and I couldn't carry it.
   B My bag was _____ heavy I couldn't carry it.

3 **A** I don't know anybody in Manchester.
   B I _____ nobody in Manchester.

4 **A** Janet spent a lot of money on holiday and now she wants to borrow some.
   B Janet spent _____ a lot of money on holiday that now she wants to borrow some.

28

The in place names

Names for places including *the*

In this unit you learn which nouns to use **the** with.

Proper nouns

Proper nouns are nouns that refer to particular named people, places or things. They are always spelled with a capital letter.

> We spent a day in **New York** and saw **the Statue of Liberty**.
> I saw **Jenny** on **Saturday**.
> He was born in **Poland** but later moved to **France**.

Some proper nouns are used with **the** and others are not. We call this the zero article.

Category	The	Zero article
Continents	—	Africa Australia
Deserts, oceans and rivers	the Gobi desert the (river) Nile the Atlantic (ocean)	—
Cities and streets	—	San Francisco Park Street Seventh Avenue
Mountains and lakes	—	Lake Superior Mount Everest
Unique buildings or attractions	the Pyramids the Eiffel Tower the Taj Mahal the Tate Gallery	—

Countries

You do not use **the** with the names of most countries. There are some where you do however and you need to remember these. Notice that you use **the** with countries that are states, kingdoms and republics or with plural nouns.

The	Zero article
The USA	Canada
The UK	Indonesia
The Maldives	France
The Netherlands	Russia
The Czech Republic	Germany

Remember!

You say **North Africa**, **East Anglia** but **the North** and **the East**.

Talking about buildings

When you know that the person you are talking or writing to will understand which thing you are referring to, you use **the**. For example, if there is only one station in a town, the people who live in the town will talk about **the station**. Similarly, people working for the same organization might talk about **the boss** or **the office** without needing to specify the organization.

> *A: How do I get to **the station**?*
> *B: You go past **the university** and turn left after **the church**.*

You also say **the doctor's** and **the baker's**. However, you don't usually use **the** when talking about going to church, work, hospital, school or university as an activity rather than a building.

> *I was **at school** with her.*
> *I go **to university** in London.*

Exercise 1

Are the highlighted words correct or incorrect in the sentences?

1 The cinema is on **the** ☐ Park Street, next to the supermarket.

2 **The** ☐ Government is increasing the price of petrol again.

3 The total number of people applying to go to **the** ☐ university in Britain has fallen this year.

4 Can you take me to **the** ☐ doctor's please? I don't feel very well.

5 The taxi will arrive at 2 p.m. to take you to **the** ☐ airport.

6 What time do you get to **the** ☐ work every day?

Exercise 2

Are the highlighted words correct or incorrect in this text?

A priceless collection of jewellery has been stolen from **the** ☐ Argento gallery, in **the** ☐ Grantham Road in the city of **the** ☐ Chesterfield. **The** ☐ police are asking people to contact them if they saw anyone behaving suspiciously in **the** ☐ city centre between the hours of 8 and 10 p.m. last night. **The** ☐ Police Inspector Karen Ward said, 'We think the criminals escaped across **the** ☐ Chandler's Park and got to **the** ☐ railway station at around 10.30 p.m. There is a reward of £1,000 for anyone who can give us useful information about where the criminals might be.' The jewellery, originally from **the** ☐ Middle East, will be very difficult to sell as it is so famous. The criminals responsible are likely to go to **the** ☐ prison for a very long time.

Exercise 3

Put each sentence into the correct order.

1 largest continent / is / in the / Asia / world. / the

_____

2 Africa / is / the / in / Sahara desert / .

_____

3 Richmond Park / UK is near / in / Wimbledon / the / .

_____

4 pyramids. / on a trip along / river Nile in / you might see the / the / Egypt,

_____

5 is the / the / Mount Etna, in / second most / active volcano in the world. / south of Italy,

_____

6 Brazil is / in / the / South America / biggest country / .

_____

Exercise 4

Choose the correct word or phrase.

1 There are 50 states in **the USA / USA**.

2 The hottest part of Spain is generally **south / the south**, near Seville.

3 The tallest building in **UK / the UK** is called the Shard and it's in London.

4 Lake Baikal in **Siberia / the Siberia** is the oldest and deepest lake in the world.

5 **The Red Sea / Red Sea** is the world's saltiest sea.

6 A lot of people enjoy sailing on **Lake Garda / the Lake Garda**.

Exercise 5

Which sentences are correct?

1 My journey from the work takes about two hours. ❑

2 His family are very religious. They go to church every week. ❑

3 If you're tired, you should go to the bed, not stay up late reading. ❑

4 Jim has gone to railway station but he'll be back soon. ❑

5 I used to play the piano but I haven't got time these days. ❑

6 Sherwood Forest in England is famous for the Robin Hood. ❑ ❑ ❑

29

Verbs + *to* or *-ing*

Using *to* or *-ing* after verbs to make different meanings

In this unit you learn how some verbs have different meanings when they are followed by **to** or *-ing*.

No difference in meaning

The following verbs can be followed by a **to**-*infinitive* clause or an *-ing* clause, with little difference in meaning: **attempt, begin, bother, continue, fear, hate, love, prefer, start, try**

> *It started **raining**.*
> *A very cold wind had started **to blow**.*
> *The captain didn't bother **answering**.*
> *I didn't bother **to answer**.*

Note that if these verbs are used in the continuous, they are followed by a **to**-*infinitive* clause.

> *The company is beginning **to export** to the West.*
> *We are continuing **to make** good progress.*

> ### Remember!
>
> After **begin**, **continue** and **start**, you use a **to**-*infinitive* clause with the verbs **understand**, **know** and **realize**.
> *I began **to understand** her a bit better.*

Some difference in meaning

Like

You can often use **like** with a **to**-*infinitive* or an *-ing* clause with little difference in meaning.

> *I like **to fish**.*
> *I like **fishing**.*

However, there is sometimes a difference. You can use **like** followed by a **to**-*infinitive* clause to say that you think something is a good idea, or the right thing to do. You cannot use an *-ing* clause with this meaning.

> *They like **to interview** people first.*
> *I didn't like **to ask** him.*

Remember, forget, regret

After **remember**, **forget** and **regret**, you use an **-ing** clause if you are referring to an event after it has happened.

> *I remember **discussing** it once before.*
> *I'll never forget **seeing** the Taj Mahal.*
> *She did not regret **accepting** his offer.*

You use a **to**-*infinitive* clause after **remember** and **forget** if you are referring to an event before it happens.

> *I must remember **to call** Dad tonight.*
> *Don't forget **to send** in your entries.*

After **regret**, in formal English, you use a **to**-*infinitive* clause with these verbs to say that you are sorry about what you are saying or doing now: **announce**, **inform**, **learn**, **say**, **see**, **tell**

> *We regret **to announce** that the London train has been cancelled.*

Try

If you **try to do** something, you make an effort to do it. If you **try doing** something, you do it as an experiment, for example to see if you like it or if it is effective.

> *I tried **to explain**.*
> *I tried **running** but found it boring.*

Exercise 1

Which sentences are correct?

1 I meant to call you, I promise, but I've been very busy. ❑
2 I hate to see you looking so worried. Can I help? ❑
3 My teacher really helped me learning English. ❑
4 Finally, after weeks of lessons, they began to understand a little French. ❑
5 Stop to shout! I hate the noise! ❑
6 We really like you staying at our house. ❑

Exercise 2

Are the highlighted words correct or incorrect in the sentences?

1 My son forgot **feeding** ❑ the cats, so they were very hungry when I got home.
2 Everyone started **running** ❑ when they saw the bus.
3 I've tried not **eating** ❑ so much but I always feel hungry.
4 Generally speaking, I like **to swim** ❑ in the afternoon.
5 You need **helping** ❑ me because I can't do it alone.
6 They all started **to laugh** ❑ when they saw my new coat.

Exercise 3

Write the infinitive or the -ing form of the verb in brackets to complete each sentence.

1 Darren stopped _____ (swim) for three months after his accident.

2 Don't worry, I always remember _____ (go) to the bank on Fridays so I won't forget this week.

3 I couldn't catch Tom and Sarah's attention – they just went on _____ (talk).

4 He needs _____ (have) a lot more driving lessons before he takes the test.

5 I'll never forget _____ (spend) long summer holidays at my grandparents' home when I was a child.

6 He failed his law exams three times but he went on _____ (try) until finally he passed.

Exercise 4

Write the missing words in sentence B so that it means the same as sentence A.

1 **A** I don't shop at that supermarket any more because it's too expensive.
  B I've stopped _____ at that supermarket because it's too expensive.

2 **A** He should do a lot more practice if he wants to play the piano well.
  B He needs _____ a lot more practice if he wants to play the piano well.

3 **A** They still lived at the same address even though they didn't like the house.
  B They went on _____ at the same address even though they didn't like the house.

4 **A** I'm so sorry! I feel terrible because I didn't tell you about the party.
  B I regret not _____ you about the party.

Exercise 5

Are the highlighted words correct or incorrect in this text?

Dear Suzi, Janey and Soph

Sorry that this is a group email but if I try **writing** ❑ to each of you, it will take all year! I generally hate **receiving** ❑ this kind of email so I hope you won't mind too much. Listen, I need **telling** ❑ you something – I'm getting married! I started **seeing** ❑ Frank three months ago and after a week we started **to see** ❑ each other every day. I can't stop **to think** ❑ about him, when I wake up, when I go to sleep – I think about him all day!

So, here's the question. Will you three be at the wedding? It's on the 17th of next month. Please say yes!

Paulette

x

Exercise 6

Decide if the pairs of sentences have the same meaning.

1 **A** I remembered to send Maggie an email.
  B I remembered sending Maggie an email. ☐

2 **A** He prefers going to the gym on Sundays because it's not crowded.
  B He prefers to go to the gym on Sundays because it's not crowded. ☐

3 **A** I regret to say that your application was not successful.
  B I regret saying that your application was not successful. ☐

4 **A** She stopped listening to the man singing in the street.
  B She stopped to listen to the man singing in the street. ☐

5 **A** They continued to dance after the music stopped.
  B They continued dancing after the music stopped. ☐

Exercise 7

For each sentence, tick the correct ending.

1 Just as we were about to leave the house,
  ☐ it started to rain.
  ☐ it started to have rained.
  ☐ it started to be raining.

2 It was only when I took him to the airport
  ☐ that I began to be realizing that I might never see him again.
  ☐ that I began to realize that I might never see him again.
  ☐ that I began realizing that I might never see him again.

3 Jorge is happy at school now,
  ☐ and his confidence is continuing growing.
  ☐ and his confidence is continuing to grow.
  ☐ and his confidence is continuing to be growing.

4 Please don't forget
  ☐ to have bought some milk on your way home.
  ☐ buying some milk on your way home.
  ☐ to buy some milk on your way home.

5 The children will never forget
  ☐ to go to Lapland to meet Father Christmas.
  ☐ going to Lapland to meet Father Christmas.
  ☐ to be going to Lapland to meet Father Christmas.

6 We regret
  ☐ telling you that your application has not been successful.
  ☐ to be telling you that your application has not been successful.
  ☐ to tell you that your application has not been successful.

30

Giving short answers to questions
so and *neither*

In this unit you learn how to give short answers, using **so** and **neither**.

> | | |
> |---|---|
> | **Sarah** | I'm excited! |
> | **Christine** | So am I! |
> | **Sarah** | I've never seen One Love live before. |
> | **Christine** | Neither have I! |

So and *neither*

Sometimes a statement about one person also applies to another person. When this is the case, you can use a short answer with **so** for positive statements, and with **neither** or **nor** for negative statements.

A: You were different then.
*B: **So** were you.*

A: I don't usually have breakfast.
*B: **Neither** do I.*

A: I can't do it.
*B: **Nor** can I.*

You can use **not either** instead of **neither**, in which case the verb comes after the subject.

A: He doesn't understand.
*B: We **don't either**.*

You use the same verb that was used in the statement. The verb comes before the subject. Where there is no auxiliary or modal verb you use **do**.

A: *I can't see him.*
B: *Neither **can** I.*

A: *I play a lot of sports.*
B: *So **do** I.*

A: *Alex wasn't at the party.*
B: *Nor **was** David.*

Exercise 1

Match the two parts.

1 I've never been to the USA on holiday.
2 I'm thinking of applying for that job in the newspaper.
3 I'm not going to the concert; it's too expensive.
4 I hadn't met Nathan until last week.
5 I was asleep when we had that earthquake the other night.

a Nor had I.
b Neither have I.
c So am I.
d So was I.
e Neither am I.

Exercise 2

For each question, tick the correct answer.

1 If I've got to visit Jamie and Sam, then
   ❑ so did you.
   ❑ so have you.
   ❑ so are you.

2 Customers didn't notice the shoplifter and
   ❑ neither did the security guard.
   ❑ neither had the security guard.
   ❑ nor has the security guard.

3 Neither the bride's family
   ❑ so the groom's attended the wedding.
   ❑ nor the groom's attended the wedding.
   ❑ either the groom's attended the wedding.

4 The head of human resources has resigned and
   ❑ nor has the head of recruitment.
   ❑ neither has the head of recruitment.
   ❑ so has the head of recruitment.

5 You shouldn't drink anything before the operation and
   ❑ neither should you eat anything.
   ❑ nor you should eat anything.
   ❑ so should you eat anything.

Exercise 3

Complete the text by writing one word in each gap.

Ben: What's wrong, Helen? You look stressed out. You're supposed to be having fun, you know – we're buying your birthday present!

Helen: I know, but I'm hopeless at technology. All these cameras are the same. Look, this one takes 16 megapixel photographs and so [1]_____ this one.

Ben: Ah, but that one doesn't have an optical zoom and this one does.

Helen: I'm not sure I like either of them, actually. [2]_____ of them comes in a range of colours, just black. It's a bit boring.

Ben: Oh, Helen. It's the quality of the photo that counts. Look, how about one of these two? Let's see, this one can be programmed to take photos automatically and so [3]_____ this one. This more expensive model has won an award.

Helen: But so [4]_____ the cheaper model.

Ben: Not really. It's just that the cheaper one is 'star buy of the month' in the store.

Helen: Look, do we both really need a camera? If I'm taking photos of everything on holiday and so [5]_____ you, we're both going to have exactly the same photographs. It's pointless!

Ben: But what about that photography course? I was really looking forward to that and so [6]_____ you, I thought.

Helen: I'm having second thoughts about that, Ben. The course is really expensive. Neither you [7]_____ I can really afford it.

Ben: OK, so you don't want to buy a camera, and after all that, neither [8]_____ I! How about that pair of shoes you had your eye on instead?

Exercise 4

Which sentences are correct?

1 Terry wasn't convinced that he could justify the cost of the holiday and so wasn't Isla. ❑

2 The city mayor wouldn't consider the housing development and nor would the local council. ❑

3 Paul should have sent his father a birthday card and so had Sarah. ❑

4 You wouldn't wear jeans to a job interview and neither would I. ❑

5 Knives and forks can be found on the end table and so are serviettes. ❑

6 My family all have red hair and so does my husband's. ❑

Exercise 5

Are the highlighted words and phrases correct or incorrect in the sentences?

1 I've been to France several times, and **so did** ❑ Maria.

2 I should go home before it gets dark, and **so should** ❑ you.

3 The tennis club's president hasn't won any competitions and **nor has** ❑ the secretary.

4 I've lived in London for over 30 years and **so was** ❑ my brother.

5 My parents are quite up-to-date, but neither of them **don't like** ❑ reading newspapers online.

6 Stephen used to live in Egypt, and so **used to** ❑ his brother, Bob.

Exercise 6

Complete the sentences by writing one word in each gap.

1 Carlos has got dark wavy hair and so _____ his brother Miguel.

2 _____ Carlos nor Miguel likes living in the countryside.

3 Miguel doesn't like studying English and nor _____ Carlos.

4 Miguel has been playing football since he was young and so _____ Carlos.

5 Carlos would like to get married one day and so _____ Miguel.

6 Miguel doesn't have any idea what job he wants to do and nor _____ Carlos.

Exercise 7

Decide if the pairs of sentences have the same meaning.

1 **A** Pablo likes to have coffee with his breakfast and so does Susan.
  B Both Pablo and Susan like to have coffee with their breakfast. ❑

2 **A** I don't know what I'm getting for Christmas, and neither does my sister.
  B I only know what my sister is getting me for Christmas. ❑

3 **A** Giuseppe can't speak French, and neither can I.
  B I am better at speaking French than Giuseppe. ❑

4 **A** Ali doesn't want to go to the party, and Dan doesn't either.
  B Neither Ali nor Dan wants to go to the party. ❑

5 **A** Carla can play tennis really well, and so can her brother.
  B Both Carla and her brother can play tennis really well. ❑

6 **A** Henry didn't enjoy the day out and nor did Pierre.
  B Pierre enjoyed the day out but Henry didn't. ❑

Answer key

1 Past simple, present perfect and present perfect continuous

Exercise 1

1 gone	3 written	5 've
2 Did	4 I've lived	6 did

Exercise 2

1 Yes	3 Yes	5 No
2 No	4 Yes	6 No

Exercise 3

1 I've been doing. ✓	4 I've been going ✓
2 I've been ✓	5 didn't go ✓
3 didn't seem ✗	6 ate ✗

Exercise 4

1 Yes	3 No
2 Yes	4 Yes

Exercise 5

1 've studied *or* have studied

2 lived

3 spoke

4 was

5 've worked *or* have worked

6 visited

Exercise 6

1 d	3 b	5 e
2 a	4 c	6 f

2 Past perfect, past perfect continuous and present perfect continuous

Exercise 1

1 have	4 I'd been
2 I've been calling	5 hadn't bought
3 has been looking	6 had been

Exercise 2

1 c	3 d	5 b
2 f	4 e	6 a

Exercise 3

1 I'd been sleeping

2 I'd overslept

3 Have you been sleeping

4 I'd missed

5 She'd been joking

6 I'd been cleaning

Exercise 4

1 been	3 been	5 had
2 had	4 looking	6 had

Exercise 5

1 doing	3 had	5 have
2 tried	4 appeared	6 feeling

Exercise 6

1 Archie realised he hadn't been cycling for ages, so he decided to go that afternoon.

2 It hadn't stopped raining for a month and everyone was really fed up.

3 Jo had forgotten to buy her daughter the computer game she wanted, even though she'd put it on her shopping list.

4 You look hot! Have you been out running?

5 Morag hadn't uploaded her work onto the website and her teacher was really annoyed.

6 I haven't been practising recently and I can hardly remember how to play my violin.

Exercise 7

1 No	3 Yes	5 No
2 No	4 Yes	

Exercise 8

1 Yes	3 Yes	5 No
2 No	4 No	6 Yes

3 Modals and passives

Exercise 1

1 must have been paid by now.

2 used to be ridden for two hours a day.

3 to be built on the site this year.

4 he should have been promoted this year.

5 will be arrested.

Exercise 2

1 be locked	4 have been completed
2 to be eaten	5 should be given
3 to be worn	

Exercise 3

1	be	4	should	7	will
2	used	5	can		
3	wouldn't	6	can't		

Exercise 4

1	No	3	Yes	5	No
2	No	4	No	6	Yes

Exercise 5

1	Yes	3	Yes	5	No
2	No	4	No		

Exercise 6

1 A celebrity may be offered a lot of money to write their autobiography.

2 That letter can't be meant for you – it hasn't got your name on it.

3 Alexander should have been taught English from an earlier age; it's harder to learn when you're older.

4 Tomorrow, the bride and groom will be brought to the hotel by chauffeur-driven limousine.

5 Cassie should not have been released from hospital today; she still feels unwell.

6 A complimentary ticket to our next event will be given out to the first 200 people through the doors.

Exercise 7

1	have ✓	3	mustn't ✓	5	hasn't ✗
2	have ✓	4	had ✓	6	been ✗

Exercise 8

1 may have been spent

2 should be taken out

3 used to be hired

4 can be learned

Exercise 9

1	have	3	didn't	5	can't
2	have	4	be	6	have

Exercise 10

1	can be	4	shouldn't be
2	may have been	5	didn't used to be
3	going to be	6	could be

4 It sentences

Exercise 1

1	Going out	3	It wasn't
2	to finish	4	Is it better

Exercise 2

1	Yes	4	Yes
2	No	5	Yes
3	Yes		

Exercise 3

1	to see	4	to eat
2	nicer	5	for them
3	for me		

Exercise 4

1	to come	4	for
2	to be	5	came to visit
3	to go		

Exercise 5

1 Was it possible for the children to play outside?

2 It's not good for you to be working so hard.

3 It must be nice for them to see you again.

4 It wasn't hard for her to finish on time.

5 It's much easier for me to do that for you.

6 It isn't always possible for me to call.

Exercise 6

1	Yes	3	Yes	5	Yes
2	No	4	No	6	Yes

5 Reporting statements and imperatives

Exercise 1

1	f	3	a	5	d
2	c	4	b	6	e

Exercise 2

1	promised	4	suggested
2	insisted	5	told
3	warned	6	encouraged

Exercise 3

1	No	3	Yes	5	No
2	Yes	4	No		

Exercise 4

1	apologized ✗	4	told ✗
2	offered ✓	5	reminded ✗
3	advised ✓	6	refused ✓

Exercise 5

1 Steffi agreed to go bungee jumping with me. I'm so glad we did it!

2 'Be careful with that hot coffee!' she warned us.

3 Petra insisted that we stayed for dinner.

4 Nicole suggested going to the aerobics class with her.

5 Mum promised to go shopping with me later that day.

6 Candice encouraged her brother to buy the new car he wanted.

Exercise 6

1 the previous

2 that

3 there

4 the previous day

5 the following week

6 the day before

Exercise 7

1 Andrew admitted breaking my bike.

2 They told me I hadn't got the job.

3 Penelope decided not to go to the barbecue.

4 Bradley agreed to go to the hospital with me.

5 Pat apologized for what he had said.

6 The waiter recommended a good wine.

Exercise 8

1 that	3 me	5 to
2 me	4 not	6 on

Exercise 9

1 told

2 to meet

3 explained

4 reminded us

5 taking

6 to help

6 Reporting questions

Exercise 1

1 Yes	3 Yes	5 Yes
2 No	4 No	6 No

Exercise 2

1 Yolanda wondered if she had time to wash her hair before she went out.

2 Sergio wanted the sales assistant to tell him what time the shop closed.

3 He asked me if I knew where his car keys were.

4 Michelle wondered whether she could afford the new dress she had seen.

5 Pietro wanted to know how much the holiday to Majorca cost.

6 She asked me what I thought about the movie.

Exercise 3

1 d	3 f	5 a
2 c	4 b	6 e

Exercise 4

1 couldn't

2 was

3 wanted

4 whether

Exercise 5

1 No	4 Yes
2 Yes	5 No
3 Yes	

Exercise 6

1 would be	4 would have
2 asked	5 wanted
3 had seen	6 had done

Exercise 7

1 whether I still lived in Oxford.

2 why Maria hadn't told him about her new job.

3 and demanded to know who I had been out with that night.

4 whether I had seen the robbers entering the bank.

5 how long he'd been planning her birthday party.

7 Modals (1)

Exercise 1

1 d	3 a	5 c
2 f	4 b	6 e

Exercise 2

1 a	3 d	5 c
2 e	4 f	6 b

Exercise 3

1 is going to climb	4 is going to make
2 are going to be	5 am going to find
3 are going to have	6 are going to love

Exercise 4

1 decided	3 Will
2 Let's	4 will

Exercise 5

1 I shall be so happy when my exams finish.

2 Why won't you say what's wrong?

3 How will you get home after the party?

4 I'll probably spend my birthday money on some new jeans.

5 Everyone will be amazed at our news.

6 We'll be sad when you leave the office.

8 Used to

Exercise 1

1 used	5 used
2 used to	6 used
3 used to freeze	7 didn't use
4 didn't use	

Exercise 2

1 didn't use to ✓	4 use to work ✗
2 doesn't use to ✗	5 Don't you use to ✗
3 Did you use to ✓	6 Have you used to ✗

Exercise 3

1 didn't you use to go
2 did you use to like
3 used to be
4 didn't use to understand
5 did Mary use to have
6 used to look after

Exercise 4

1 No   3 No   5 Yes
2 Yes   4 No   6 Yes

Exercise 5

1 used to   3 used to   5 used to
2 use to   4 didn't use to 6 use to

Exercise 6

1 Women didn't use to be allowed to vote.
2 Gloria used to visit us every week.
3 I didn't use to like running.
4 Didn't you use to live in a flat?
5 My brother and I used to stand on the bridge and wave at the trains.
6 Did you use to get up early?

9 Modals (2)

Exercise 1

1 d   2 f   3 b   4 c   5 a   6 e

Exercise 2

1 Yes   3 Yes   5 No
2 No   4 Yes   6 No

Exercise 3

1 don't have to   3 need to   5 have
2 need to   4 have to   6 must

Exercise 4

1 No   3 Yes   5 Yes
2 No   4 No

Exercise 5

1 mustn't   3 had to   5 needs
2 don't have   4 must   6 needn't

Exercise 6

1 We don't need any more offers of help.
2 You mustn't eat any more chocolates.
3 Trevor has to be home by 9 o'clock.
4 Sarah didn't need to do all the cooking herself – I'd offered to help her.
5 You must have a break before you do any more work.
6 The kitchen needs to be cleaned thoroughly.

Exercise 7

1 needn't ✓   4 didn't have to ✓
2 didn't need to ✓ 5 needn't ✗
3 need ✗   6 don't must ✗

Exercise 8

1 The train will be late so we needn't hurry.
2 The company has to decide which product to develop.
3 You must email me as soon as your exam results arrive.
4 The team needs to attract more supporters.
5 We mustn't forget to buy some souvenirs.
6 Do we have to leave so early?

Exercise 9

1 Yes   3 No   5 No
2 Yes   4 Yes   6 Yes

10 Modals (3)

Exercise 1

1 e   2 b   3 d   4 f   5 a   6 c

Exercise 2

1 must   3 must   5 could
2 might   4 can't   6 can't

Exercise 3

1 must ✓   3 might ✗   5 might ✓
2 could ✓ 4 must ✗   6 can't ✓

Exercise 4

1 He might be stuck in traffic.
2 Sara must be at least 30.
3 I suppose he could be her son.
4 She might be Maria's sister.
5 He can't be the driver of the car.
6 He must be the owner of the shop.

Exercise 5

1 Yes   3 Yes   5 No
2 No   4 Yes

Exercise 6

1 No   3 Yes   5 Yes
2 Yes   4 No   6 No

11 Showing how certain you are about situations

Exercise 1

1 may   3 prefer
2 fairly   4 not

Exercise 2

1 could ✓   4 might ✓
2 must ✗   5 having ✗
3 may ✓   6 to ✗

Exercise 3

1 would rather	4 prefer
2 sure	5 obvious
3 know	6 rather

Exercise 4

1 I am fairly sure I had £10 in my purse. I wonder where I spent it.

2 I think it's going to snow; it's getting colder and colder.

3 I will buy those shoes after all. I am absolutely sure they will look great with my blue dress.

4 What would you prefer doing tonight? Shall we go to the cinema or stay at home and watch TV?

5 I think I would quite like to learn how to make my own clothes, so I may do a course at the college.

6 I would rather not come to the shopping mall with you; it will be so busy on a Saturday.

Exercise 5

1 Yes	3 No	5 No
2 Yes	4 No	

Exercise 6

1 Yes	3 Yes	5 Yes
2 No	4 No	6 No

Exercise 7

1 I believe I'm always right!

2 Jenny may win the competition after all that practice.

3 It's clear you need some help with your homework.

4 I'm absolutely sure I gave you this book last Christmas.

5 I would rather get a taxi than walk.

6 What would you prefer for dinner, chicken or fish?

Exercise 8

1 b	2 a	3 d	4 e	5 f	6 c

Exercise 9

1 know	3 going	5 rather
2 absolutely	4 may	6 prefer

12 Second and third conditionals

Exercise 1

1 a	2 e	3 f	4 b	5 d	6 c

Exercise 2

1 hadn't ✓	4 forgot ✗
2 have ✗	5 argued ✗
3 have ✗	6 had ✓

Exercise 3

1 I wouldn't sunbathe in the hot sun unless I wore a lot of suntan lotion.

2 If Marco hadn't studied so hard, he wouldn't have got such good grades in the exam.

3 If you'd like to accept the job, I would be delighted to hire you.

4 Laura wouldn't have met Andy if they hadn't worked at the same company.

5 If London hadn't won the 2012 Olympic bid, poor parts of the city wouldn't have been rebuilt.

6 They would go abroad more on holiday if Sue would let someone look after the dog.

Exercise 4

1 Yes	3 No	5 No
2 No	4 No	

Exercise 5

1 hadn't	4 wanted
2 would have	5 wouldn't be
3 would win	

Exercise 6

1 If Michelangelo hadn't painted the Sistine Chapel, he wouldn't have become one of the most famous artists of all time.

2 If you had the money, would you buy a house abroad?

3 If Tim got the professional position he applied for, we'd all miss him.

4 There would be less crime if unemployment wasn't so high.

5 I wouldn't have asked her out unless you had told me that it was OK.

6 Gemma wouldn't be so fit if she didn't have a personal trainer.

Exercise 7

1 Yes	3 No	5 Yes
2 No	4 No	6 Yes

Exercise 8

1 asked	5 hadn't	9 was or were
2 would	6 would	10 wouldn't
3 would	7 hadn't	11 Would
4 unless	8 wouldn't	

13 Conditionals

Exercise 1

1 look after the kids tomorrow.

2 will he go to university?

3 she hadn't eaten in weeks.

4 I'll let you go out tonight.

5 I had enough money for the plane ticket.

Exercise 2

1 answer
2 don't
3 found
4 would you
5 wouldn't
6 would the police know
7 was
8 would

Exercise 3

1 have
2 hadn't
3 if
4 as
5 supposing
6 provided
7 had
8 couldn't
9 long

Exercise 4

1 Providing that you travel outside rush hour, public transport won't be too busy.

2 If Abdul had told Leyla how he felt, she wouldn't have gone away.

3 Global warming will be reduced as long as we stop using so much energy.

4 Supposing it was sunny every day, would people miss rain?

5 If Britain didn't have a monarchy, the tourist industry would suffer.

6 As long as you treat people kindly, they will treat you the same way.

Exercise 5

1 Supposed ✗
2 Provided ✓
3 would ✗
4 as ✗
5 in ✗
6 through ✗
7 aren't ✗

Exercise 6

1 No
2 No
3 Yes
4 No
5 No
6 Yes

Exercise 7

1 Yes
2 No
3 Yes
4 No
5 No

Exercise 8

1 As long
2 Supposing
3 condition that
4 Supposing

14 Present simple and present perfect in future time

Exercise 1

1 Yes
2 Yes
3 No
4 Yes
5 No
6 Yes

Exercise 2

1 a
2 c
3 d
4 e
5 b
6 f

Exercise 3

1 leave ✓
2 has checked ✓
3 will arrive ✗
4 will end ✗
5 has had ✓
6 has apologized ✓

Exercise 4

1 is
2 will be
3 has left
4 will see
5 has seen
6 will leave

Exercise 5

1 will end
2 is
3 will leave
4 will make
5 will reach
6 arrives
7 will finish
8 cycles

Exercise 6

1 have washed
2 will enjoy
3 am
4 arrives
5 will apply
6 have repaired

15 Adverbs

Exercise 1

1 still
2 any more
3 still
4 yet
5 only

Exercise 2

1 Yes
2 No
3 Yes
4 No

Exercise 3

1 any more
2 even
3 still
4 yet
5 only
6 no longer

Exercise 4

1 Some people even walked out because the film was so boring.

2 I'm still waiting to hear about the job I applied for.

3 I've decided I don't want to play volleyball any more.

4 Why haven't the children gone to bed yet?

5 Students were only allowed into the sports centre with a coach.

6 We couldn't stay any longer because we had to catch our bus.

Exercise 5

1 No
2 Yes
3 Yes
4 No
5 Yes
6 No

Exercise 6

1 yet ✗
2 Even ✗
3 any longer ✓
4 any more ✗
5 still ✓
6 only ✓

Exercise 7

1 but she still wouldn't tell me where she'd been.

2 and it still isn't finished.

3 but they haven't set a date for their wedding yet.

4 we still haven't agreed the terms of the contract.

5 had her baby yet?

6 they were still paying off their debts.

16 Asking for, giving and refusing permission

Exercise 1

1 all right	**3** mind	**5** for
2 rather	**4** afraid	**6** to

Exercise 2

1 Yes, of course.

2 Sure. Please do.

3 I'd rather you didn't.

4 I'm afraid that's not possible.

5 No, not at all.

6 Yes, go ahead.

Exercise 3

1 Is it	**3** May	**5** Could you
2 Would	**4** Are we	**6** Is it

Exercise 4

1 would	**3** could	**5** mind
2 is	**4** course	**6** afraid

Exercise 5

1 Yes	**3** No	**5** No
2 No	**4** Yes	**6** Yes

Exercise 6

1 Would you mind if I opened the gate?

2 May I leave the room?

3 Would you mind helping me?

4 Is it OK if I wait outside?

5 Could I have a look at your photos?

6 Can I borrow your mobile?

Exercise 7

1 didn't	**3** not	**5** go
2 course	**4** afraid	**6** fine

Exercise 8

1 a   **2** f   **3** d   **4** b   **5** e   **6** c

17 Comparatives

Exercise 1

1 Yes	**3** Yes	**5** No
2 No	**4** Yes	**6** No

Exercise 2

1 much	**3** cooler	**5** further
2 as	**4** more	**6** than

Exercise 3

1 No	**3** No	**5** Yes
2 Yes	**4** No	**6** Yes

Exercise 4

1 Paula ran as fast as possible.

2 John is not as tall as his brother.

3 Many more people went to this year's festival.

4 The weather will be much worse than last year.

5 The film was better than I expected it to be.

6 Why is there more litter in the park than before?

Exercise 5

1 Mark travels much further to work than I do.

2 Today's lesson wasn't so interesting as yesterday's.

3 The new teacher explains things much more clearly.

4 This pizza is tastier than the one I had last week.

5 More people are taking a winter holiday now than ten years ago.

6 How much longer will we have to wait?

Exercise 6

1 tidier	**4** more intelligent
2 worse	**5** well
3 quickly	**6** better

18 Adjective order

Exercise 1

1 and	**3** patient	**5** sandy
2 comfortable	**4** easy	**6** or

Exercise 2

1 Mary bought a new yellow jacket yesterday.

2 Look at those big black clouds!

3 We saw a beautiful round wooden table in that shop.

4 Why did Ann look sad and upset yesterday?

5 Have you seen my black leather gloves?

6 Sarah is the woman with the beautiful long black hair.

Exercise 3

1 Yes	**3** Yes	**5** No
2 No	**4** Yes	**6** No

Exercise 4

1 Tony is really easy-going and relaxed.

2 Which flavour yoghurt would you like, blueberry or strawberry?

3 Who is that tall woman, the one with the large blue eyes?

4 The food in that restaurant isn't good or cheap.

5 The most important thing is for you to feel calm, relaxed and happy.

6 I didn't like that film because it was long and boring.

Exercise 5

1 French	**3** and	**5** brown
2 and	**4** or	

Exercise 6

| **1** f | **2** e | **3** c | **4** d | **5** b | **6** a |

19 -ing/-ed adjectives

Exercise 1

| **1** c | **2** a | **3** f | **4** e | **5** d | **6** b |

Exercise 2

1 interesting	**4** excited
2 amazing	**5** disappointing
3 annoyed	**6** frightened

Exercise 3

1 to see me.	**4** to do the work.
2 he'd failed.	**5** to hear the news.
3 to ask for help.	**6** surprised to see what happened.

Exercise 4

1 Harry watched an amazing match on TV.

2 Karen was afraid to ask for help.

3 This is a very boring film.

4 It is interesting to visit the museum.

5 Was it an exciting game?

6 Tim was shocked to hear the news.

Exercise 5

1 exciting.	**4** to give me some help.
2 shocked.	**5** tiring.
3 frightening.	**6** to see me.

20 Using -ing forms as nouns

Exercise 1

1 Playing	**3** talking
2 coming	**4** Driving

Exercise 2

1 smoking	**3** flying	**5** taking
2 reading	**4** opening	**6** doing

Exercise 3

1 To dance ✗	**5** talk ✗
2 Moving ✓	**6** spend ✗
3 to go ✗	**7** to help ✓
4 exercising ✓	

Exercise 4

1 It's late. Let's finish cleaning the house tomorrow.

2 How often have I told you to stop playing that guitar at night?

3 Spending all your money on holiday like this is not a good idea.

4 Please continue playing the piano. I love listening to the music.

5 Don't talk to me about Joan. Just seeing her makes me angry.

6 There are lots of things I enjoy doing, but cooking the dinner isn't one of them.

Exercise 5

1 Yes	**3** No	**5** Yes
2 No	**4** No	

Exercise 6

1 No	**3** Yes	**5** Yes
2 Yes	**4** No	**6** No

Exercise 7

1 All that reading isn't good for your eyes.

2 My favourite hobbies are singing and playing the piano.

3 Watching cooking programmes on TV makes me hungry.

4 Becoming a teacher was the best thing I ever did.

5 Peter suggested going to a party and I agreed.

6 Thomas loves listening to music but he hates playing it.

21 Nouns and indefinite pronouns + to-infinitive

Exercise 1

| **1** a | **2** f | **3** e | **4** d | **5** b | **6** c |

Exercise 2

1 No	**3** No	**5** Yes
2 Yes	**4** Yes	**6** No

Exercise 3

1 to	**5** to
2 dance	**6** anything
3 to ask	**7** to
4 to remember	

Exercise 4

1 You need a friend to talk to when you have a problem.

2 The desert in the south west is an interesting area to visit.

3 I've got nothing to add to my previous statement.

4 Can you give anything to help the homeless?

5 In my opinion, it's a good business to invest in.

6 Is there anything to put rubbish in?

Exercise 5

1 somewhere	3 advise	5 nothing
2 sit	4 to	6 something

Exercise 6

1 Yes	3 No	5 Yes
2 Yes	4 No	6 Yes

22 wh-clauses

Exercise 1

1 why	3 who	5 how
2 where	4 which	6 what

Exercise 2

1 c   2 d   3 a   4 f   5 b   6 e

Exercise 3

1 I don't know what to do.

2 I've discovered where that man works.

3 I wonder what will happen.

4 Susie explained why she was laughing.

5 I don't know which dress to buy.

6 Do you remember who said that?

Exercise 4

1 what	3 why	5 who
2 where	4 how	6 which

Exercise 5

1 No	3 Yes	5 Yes
2 Yes	4 No	6 No

Exercise 6

1 what	3 which	5 how
2 why	4 where	6 who

23 Relative pronouns

Exercise 1

1 whose	3 who	5 who
2 who	4 whose	6 whose

Exercise 2

1 York, which

2 wife, whose job is very well-paid,

3 cousin who lives by the sea

4 the city where he was born

Exercise 3

1 a   2 c   3 e   4 b   5 d   6 f

Exercise 4

1 which ✗	3 where ✗	5 where ✓
2 that ✓	4 who ✓	6 who ✗

Exercise 5

1 Yes	3 No	5 No
2 Yes	4 No	6 Yes

Exercise 6

1 where	3 whose	5 who
2 who	4 which	6 when

Exercise 7

1 whose girlfriend I met at Sally's party.

2 which reminds me of my time in Spain, that reminds me of my time in Spain.

3 who can help me, that can help me.

4 which really upset me.

24 Have/get something done

Exercise 1

1 painted	3 has	5 stolen
2 have	4 taken	6 done

Exercise 2

1 b   2 e   3 c   4 d   5 a

Exercise 3

1 No	3 Yes	5 Yes
2 Yes	4 No	6 No

Exercise 4

1 have ✓	4 got ✓
2 it ✗	5 we're having ✓
3 did ✗	6 build ✗

Exercise 5

1 got/had	3 is having/getting
2 made	4 wrapped

Exercise 6

1 Where do you get your hair done?

2 Can I have the books delivered to a different address, please?

3 My eyes are hurting – I need to get them tested.

4 Jack had a tooth taken out at the dentist's this morning.

5 You must get those shoes mended!

6 Get that sheep out of my garden!

25 Verbs that are used together

Exercise 1

1 falling	3 to be repaired	5 pulling down
2 fixing	4 to be rebuilt	6 saying

Exercise 2

1 Yes	3 No	5 No
2 No	4 Yes	

Exercise 3

1 d   2 a   3 e   4 f   5 c   6 b

Exercise 4

1 the branch to fall before it hit her.

2 want to be repainted before we sell the house.

3 the dog to bark.

4 us going to the Olympics, but we couldn't get tickets.

5 being stitched. You should have gone to the hospital.

Exercise 5

1 Those smelly football socks need to be washed.

2 This dirty floor wants cleaning.

3 Did you see the man steal the bag?

4 Tracy heard the phone ringing, but she couldn't answer it.

5 Josh wanted to get up in time to see the sun rising.

6 He missed her so much you could almost hear his heart breaking.

Exercise 6

1 being ✓	5 to put ✓
2 learning ✗	6 done ✗
3 to be heard ✗	7 tuning ✓
4 to perform ✗	

Exercise 7

1 it needs cleaning from top to bottom.

2 and your hair wants brushing.

3 hear him come in last night?

4 of jobs that need doing?

5 and she saw the children playing in the garden.

6 except that one of the drawer handles wants fixing.

26 Prepositions

Exercise 1

1 f	3 e	5 d
2 c	4 b	6 a

Exercise 2

1 as well as	3 than	5 along
2 apart	4 In addition	6 except

Exercise 3

1 It's for cutting bread.

2 It's for opening cans.

3 It's for measuring things.

4 It's for painting.

5 It's for keeping things cold.

6 It's for opening a car door.

Exercise 4

1 from ✗	3 with ✓	5 at ✗
2 than ✓	4 with ✗	6 along ✗

Exercise 5

1 as well as	3 for	5 rather than
2 in addition	4 except for	6 with

Exercise 6

1 Yes	3 No	5 No
2 No	4 Yes	6 No

Exercise 7

1 for cutting bread.

2 and then argued with his brother when he got home.

3 as well as looking after the children.

4 apart from David who ordered a slice of chocolate cake.

5 to pick the children up now rather than later.

6 with her foot.

27 Some/any/nobody/so/such

Exercise 1

1 so	3 such	5 so
2 such	4 so	6 such

Exercise 2

1 No	3 No	5 Yes
2 Yes	4 No	6 Yes

Exercise 3

1 anybody	4 anyone else
2 no one	5 nobody else
3 someone	6 someone else

Exercise 4

1 e   2 f   3 c   4 a   5 d   6 b

Exercise 5

1 so	5 so
2 so	6 Somebody
3 someone	7 someone
4 No one	

Exercise 6

1	Yes	3	Yes	5	No
2	No	4	No		

Exercise 7

1 nobody ✗   4 no one ✓
2 such ✓, anybody ✓   5 anybody ✗, such ✗
3 so ✓, somebody ✗   6 someone ✓

Exercise 8

1 was   2 so   3 know   4 such

28 The in place names

Exercise 1

1	the ✗	3	the ✗	5	the ✓
2	The ✓	4	the ✓	6	the ✗

Exercise 2

1	the ✓	5	the ✓	9	the ✓
2	the ✗	6	The ✗	10	the ✗
3	the ✗	7	the ✗		
4	The ✓	8	the ✓		

Exercise 3

1 Asia is the largest continent in the world.
2 The Sahara desert is in Africa.
3 Richmond Park in the UK is near Wimbledon.
4 On a trip along the river Nile in Egypt, you might see the pyramids.
5 Mount Etna, in the south of Italy, is the second most active volcano in the world.
6 Brazil is the biggest country in South America.

Exercise 4

1	the USA	3	the UK	5	The Red Sea
2	the south	4	Siberia	6	Lake Garda

Exercise 5

1	No	3	No	5	Yes
2	Yes	4	No	6	No

29 Verbs + to or -ing

Exercise 1

1	Yes	3	No	5	No
2	Yes	4	Yes	6	Yes

Exercise 2

1	feeding ✗	3	eating ✓	5	helping ✗
2	running ✓	4	to swim ✓	6	to laugh ✓

Exercise 3

1	swimming	3	talking	5	spending
2	to go	4	to have	6	trying

Exercise 4

1	shopping	3	living
2	to do	4	telling

Exercise 5

1	writing ✓	3	telling ✗	5	to see ✓
2	receiving ✓	4	seeing ✓	6	to think ✗

Exercise 6

1	No	3	No	5	Yes
2	Yes	4	No		

Exercise 7

1 it started to rain.
2 that I began to realize that I might never see him again.
3 and his confidence is continuing to grow.
4 to buy some milk on your way home.
5 going to Lapland to meet Father Christmas.
6 to tell you that your application has not been successful.

30 Giving short answers to questions

Exercise 1

1 b   2 c   3 e   4 a   5 d

Exercise 2

1 so have you.
2 neither did the security guard.
3 nor the groom's attended the wedding.
4 so has the head of recruitment.
5 neither should you eat anything.

Exercise 3

1	does	4	has	7	nor
2	Neither	5	are	8	do
3	can	6	were		

Exercise 4

1	No	3	No	5	No
2	Yes	4	Yes	6	Yes

Exercise 5

1	so did ✗	4	so was ✗
2	so should ✓	5	don't like ✗
3	nor has ✓	6	used to ✗

Exercise 6

1	has	3	does	5	would
2	Neither	4	has	6	does

Exercise 7

1	Yes	3	No	5	Yes
2	No	4	Yes	6	No